# PLAYS FROM VAULT 5

SOMETHING AWFUL
Tatty Hennessy

SECOND HOME
Charlotte Chimuanya

MADAME OVARY
Rosa Hesmondhalgh

TAKE CARE
Zoë Templeman-Young & Sam McLaughlin

HEROES
Isabel Dixon

T0333663

*Also Available from Nick Hern Books*

**PLAYS FROM VAULT**

EGGS
Florence Keith-Roach

MR INCREDIBLE
Camilla Whitehill

PRIMADONNA
Rosie Kellett

CORNERMEN
Oli Forsyth

RUN
Stephen Laughton

**PLAYS FROM VAULT 3**

TUMULUS
Christopher Adams

GLITTER PUNCH
Lucy Burke

BURKAS AND BACON BUTTIES
Shamia Chalabi & Sarah Henley

WIND BIT BITTER, BIT BIT BIT HER
Sami Ibrahim

THE STRONGBOX
Stephanie Jacob

**PLAYS FROM VAULT 2**

TESTAMENT
Tristan Bernays

SAVE + QUIT
Sophia Leuner

WRETCH
Rebecca Walker

THIS MUST BE THE PLACE
Brad Birch & Kenneth Emson

MAISIE SAYS SHE LOVES ME
Jimmy Osborne

**PLAYS FROM VAULT 4**

3 BILLION SECONDS
Maud Dromgoole

ALCATRAZ
Nathan Lucky Wood

COLLAPSIBLE
Margaret Perry

INSIDE VOICES
Nabilah Said

JERICHO
MALAPROP Theatre

OPEN
Christopher Adams & Timothy Allsop

THROWN
Jodi Gray

# PLAYS FROM VAULT 5

SOMETHING AWFUL
Tatty Hennessy

SECOND HOME
Charlotte Chimuanya

MADAME OVARY
Rosa Hesmondhalgh

TAKE CARE
Zoë Templeman-Young & Sam McLaughlin

HEROES
Isabel Dixon

NICK HERN BOOKS
London
www.nickhernbooks.co.uk

**A Nick Hern Book**

*Plays from VAULT 5* first published in Great Britain in 2020 as a paperback original by Nick Hern Books Limited, The Glasshouse, 49a Goldhawk Road, London W12 8QP, in association with VAULT Festival

*Something Awful* copyright © 2020 Tatty Hennessy
*Second Home* copyright © 2020 Charlotte Chimuanya
*Madame Ovary* copyright © 2020 Rosa Hesmondhalgh
*Take Care* copyright © 2020 Zoë Templeman-Young & Sam McLaughlin
*Heroes* copyright © 2020 Isabel Dixon

The authors have asserted their moral rights

Cover image by Thomas Kirk Shannon

Designed and typeset by Nick Hern Books, London
Printed and bound in Great Britain by Mimeo Ltd, Huntingdon, Cambridgeshire PE29 6XX

A CIP catalogue record for this book is available from the British Library

ISBN 978 1 84842 933 8

**CAUTION**   All rights whatsoever in these plays are strictly reserved. Requests to reproduce the texts in whole or in part should be addressed to the publisher.

**Amateur Performing Rights**   Applications for performance, including readings and excerpts, by amateurs in the English language throughout the world should be addressed to the Performing Rights Manager, Nick Hern Books, The Glasshouse, 49a Goldhawk Road, London W12 8QP, *tel* +44 (0)20 8749 4953, *email* rights@nickhernbooks.co.uk, except as follows:

*Australia*: ORiGiN Theatrical, Level 1, 213 Clarence Street, Sydney NSW 2000, *tel* +61 (2) 8514 5201, *email* enquiries@originmusic.com.au, *web* www.origintheatrical.com.au

*New Zealand:* Play Bureau, PO Box 9013, St Clair, Dunedin 9047, *tel* (3) 455 9959, *email* info@playbureau.com

**Professional Performing Rights**   Applications for performance by professionals in any medium throughout the world, should be addressed to:

*Madame Ovary*, *Second Home*, *Take Care*: Nick Hern Books in the first instance, see details above

*Heroes*: United Agents, 12-26 Lexington St, Soho, London W1F 0LE, *fax* +44 (0) 20 3214 0801, *email* info@unitedagents.co.uk

*Something Awful*: Berlin Associates, 7 Tyers Gate, London SE1 3HX, *fax* +44 (0)20 7632 5296, *email* agents@berlinassociates.com

No performance of any kind may be given unless a licence has been obtained. Applications should be made before rehearsals begin. Publication of these plays does not necessarily indicate their availability for amateur performance.

# Contents

Welcome to VAULT Festival vii

*Something Awful* by Tatty Hennessy 1

*Second Home* by Charlotte Chimuanya 49

*Madame Ovary* by Rosa Hesmondhalgh 71

*Take Care* by Zoë Templeman-Young & Sam McLaughlin 113

*Heroes* by Isabel Dixon 149

## Welcome to VAULT Festival

Theatre's a funny thing, isn't it? Being in a dark room with a bunch of strangers, being asked to give your time and attention to this moment, here, now. And in return asking for a story, a voice, a perspective on the world. Asking to be moved. To be changed. And then we disperse. To the bar to dissect. Back home to our family or friends. Back to the everyday. But for an hour or two, we have all been a part of something. We have, artists and audience alike, been a community. Part of a story that, while it may be told again, will never exist in that exact way. It's pretty exhilarating. And at VAULT Festival, there is the opportunity to have that experience, that immediacy, that joy and risk, hundreds of times through thousands of artists. That's pretty fucking incredible.

Now, more than any other time I can think of, we are questioning whose stories we are being presented with. Who has been left out of the narrative? And why? VAULT Festival is one of the increasingly rare places where artists who are traditionally underrepresented on our stages, whether that be race, background, gender, class or ability, can have their voices heard. Their stories told. Can be seen.

This year, VAULT Festival is welcoming some of the best and strongest new writing in the country. The plays published in this collection represent a fraction of the incredibly varied, raw, vibrant, urgent and playful work across the 2020 Festival. The writers in this collection have delivered unique perspectives on the world and their experiences moving through it. I could not be more proud of this collection, and of all the work presented at this year's festival. Of the risks artists are taking in this strange and scary world, and of the unfaltering belief from everyone who comes to VAULT Festival, from audiences, staff and the artists themselves in the power of art to change that world.

As always, this collection and the new writing presented in the Festival would not be possible without the ongoing support of Nick Hern Books. Their dedication and belief in writers and their willingness to platform them through the VAULT Festival has been unwavering and we are all so thankful.

So have a read. Go see these shows. Go see the rest of them. And when you're sat in that room, willing to be moved and changed, being witness to the unique power and transience of theatre, remember we're all in this together.

*Bec Martin-Williams*
*Head of Theatre and Performance*
*VAULT Festival 2020*

*This book went to press before the end of rehearsals and so the texts may differ slightly from the plays as performed.*

# SOMETHING AWFUL

Tatty Hennessy

TATTY HENNESSY

Tatty Hennessy is an award-winning playwright, dramaturg and director. She is a graduate of the Royal Court Young Writers Programme. Previous plays include *F Off* (National Youth Theatre, Udderbelly); *A Hundred Words for Snow* (Trafalgar Studios); *The Snow Queen* (Theatre N16) and *All That Lives* (Ovalhouse).

*Something Awful* was first performed at VAULT Festival, London, on 28 January 2020.

*At the time of going to print the play was still to be cast.*

| | |
|---|---|
| *Director* | Lucy Jane Atkinson |
| *Producer* | Georgie Staight |
| | Will Adolphy |
| | for Flux Theatre |
| *Lighting Designer* | Holly Ellis |
| *Stage Manager* | Bethany Pratt |
| *Sound Designer* | Sam Glossop |

**Characters**

JEL, *female, thirteen*
SOPH, *female, thirteen*
ELLIE, *female, thirteen*

/ denotes an interruption by the following character.

**Prologue**

SOPH *and* JEL *are at the computer.* SOPH *is telling a story,* JEL*'s eyes are glued to the screen.*

SOPH. I was walking home from a late class one evening. It was autumn, not really cold yet, a chill in the air, but not too bad. The streets were totally empty. I had my earphones in listening to my favourite song. And then I looked up and –

Ahead of me there was a woman. Standing in the pool of light from a lamp-post. She definitely hadn't been up ahead of me when I last looked up. She must have moved to that spot very quickly, but now she was just. Standing there. But she was just a little woman, she didn't look threatening, out for a late stroll or on her way home from work, just like me.

She had something over the lower half of her face, covering her mouth and nose. At first I couldn't process what it was but as I drew near I could see it was a white surgical mask, white elastic tucked behind her ears.

Can I help you?

I asked.

She looked sad. Her eyes. Like maybe she'd been crying. She looked up at me. And she said something. She spoke really quietly, almost in a whisper, and her voice was muffled by the mask.

Sorry?

I leaned in a little closer to hear her.

Do you think I'm beautiful?

She asked.

Right. I figured. She's just been dumped and she's out here crying feeling sorry for herself and just wants cheering up.

Poor thing. So I smile and I say:

Sure, of course you're beautiful.

And her eyes lock on to mine and she reaches up to her ear and unhooks the white elastic and pulls off the mask and

I want to throw up.

Her face is split open, two thick jagged cuts from the edges of her mouth all through her cheeks up to her ears, like a child covering their face in red lipstick. The cuts are stitched roughly together with thick black bloody twine and the scars are still wet.

How about now?

She asks.

*Suddenly, a very loud horrible noise bursts from the laptop speakers. The masked woman attacks.* JEL *screams and slams the laptop shut.*

JEL. FUCK!

SOPH *laughs,* JEL *thumps her arm, furious.*

You know I hate the jumpy ones.

**1.**

JEL *is showing* ELLIE *round the school*. SOPH *is not helping*.

JEL. Is it different to your old school? There's lots of clubs and societies and stuff. So whatever you like I'm sure you'll find something to do. After school and on lunch. And if you have a club on you can do early lunch and skip the queue so you have time. We don't really do clubs though. Want one?

*She offers a pack of Skittles. Beat.*

ELLIE. Yeah alright.

JEL. If there's something you like that there's no club for you can start one. One girl started Jewish club and on Fridays they do their own assemblies in B1 and you don't actually even have to actually be Jewish to go. And you can do extra classes and stuff. I'm doing Mandarin. My mum says Mandarin's attractive to universities because it's an employable skill for the future. And there's loads of sports teams.

ELLIE. I don't do sports.

SOPH. You look like you do sports.

ELLIE. I don't do teams.

JEL. I do gymnastics. It's alright. Our form tutor's Mr Michaels. He's alright but he's really strict on lateness and if you're late more than twice you get a pink slip / and you have to –

ELLIE. Is he fit?

JEL. Um. He's sort of. Old.

ELLIE. Are any of them fit?

JEL. Um. / I don't…

SOPH. Jel fancies Mr O'Connell.

JEL. No I don't I just like geography.

SOPH. No one likes geography.

ELLIE. Is he fit?

SOPH. He's a teacher. That's disgusting.

ELLIE. My dad speaks Chinese.

JEL. Mandarin. Really?

ELLIE. He's a pilot.

JEL. In China?

ELLIE. Everywhere. You don't just fly one place do you that'd
be pigshit. Look.

*She shows* JEL *her phone.*

JEL. He looks nice.

ELLIE. Alright, nympho.

JEL. Is it like your old school?

ELLIE. My old school was this really hardcore girls' school
where everybody goes to like Cambridge and if you weren't
a genius you got totally dicked on. One girl in the year above
killed herself.

JEL. Oh my god.

ELLIE. Yeah it was so bad, we all had to have counselling even
if we weren't sad. But I liked the school. It wasn't in the
middle of fucking nowhere.

SOPH. So why'd you move, then?

ELLIE. My dad got this huge promotion.

SOPH. A pilot promotion?

ELLIE. Yeah. Bought this big house in the country, moved us.
It was that or boarding school and boarding schools are for
lesbians and psychopaths so. There's a pool but I hate
swimming.

JEL. I love swimming.

ELLIE. You should come round and swim some time.

JEL. Do you have pool noodles?

ELLIE. Obviously. (*To* SOPH.) You swim?

SOPH. No.

ELLIE. What do you fucking do then?


**2.**

ELLIE *and* JEL *are playing a game with paper and a pen.*
SOPH *is on her laptop.*

ELLIE. Number two.

JEL. I don't know.

ELLIE. Like anything.

JEL. Like. Hug?

ELLIE. Okay. Boring. Number three?

JEL. I don't know, I don't / know what's good.

ELLIE. Like shag on a desk or shag on a pool table / or

JEL. Okay fine. Um. Yeah, shag on a desk.

ELLIE. Oh my god. Okay. Number four.

JEL. Um. Shag. In a swimming pool?

ELLIE. Yes. Okay. Five?

JEL. Um shag in the library?

ELLIE. Okay. So. You are going to stab Ms Jamil.

JEL. No!

ELLIE. Hug Soph.

JEL. Ms Jamil's so lovely.

ELLIE. Shag Mr O'Connell on a desk.

JEL. Gross.

ELLIE. Oh my god you've gone so red you love it you perv.

JEL. No.

ELLIE. Shag the Queen in a swimming pool. That's probably treason. And shag Mr Graves in the library can you imagine?

JEL. He's so hairy, it's so gross.

ELLIE. Imagine it all, like, rubbing on you.

JEL. Ew.

ELLIE. Getting stuck between your teeth.

JEL. Stop.

SOPH. Have you actually ever shagged someone?

ELLIE. Almost. My boyfriend in my old school tried but his cock was too big and it hurt too much so I just had to suck it instead.

JEL. Eew.

SOPH. That never happened.

ELLIE. Um. Yes it did.

SOPH. Sure.

ELLIE. It did. Just cos no one wants to fuck you.

JEL. You put it in your mouth?

ELLIE. It's not that bad really. And like. When you love someone it's nice to do nice things for them.

JEL. Yeah.

SOPH. What would you know?

JEL. I can imagine.

SOPH *rolls her eyes.*

JEL. Were you sad to leave him?

ELLIE. Yeah but we chat all the time and I send him pics so it's not that bad. Here, I'll show you.

JEL. No thanks.

ELLIE. I meant I'll show you him. Lezzer. God you two are freaks.

SOPH. Why are you hanging out with us then?

JEL. Soph, she's just / joking.

ELLIE. Alright, take your tampon out.

SOPH. No one's making you stay, you can go.

JEL. I want her to stay. I wanna see the photo.

SOPH *returns, pointedly, to her screen.* ELLIE *smiles, gets out her phone.*

ELLIE. This is him... Ugh, why does this shitty school block everything?

JEL. Soph can fix it for you.

ELLIE. What?

JEL. She can go on any site, even on the / school computers.

SOPH. Jel, fucksake!

JEL. What?

ELLIE. Show me.

SOPH. No.

ELLIE. Why not?

SOPH. I don't feel like it.

ELLIE. Why not?

SOPH. Oh, I don't know, cos I'm such a freak?

JEL. Soph go on.

SOPH. She'll fucking tell everyone and then / school will find out and Mr Norman will.

ELLIE. Who would I tell?

SOPH. Um, Nicola, Jenny, any of / them.

ELLIE. I would / not.

SOPH. And then they'd all want me to help them post / their dumb videos.

ELLIE. I'm not gonna, okay? Swear. On my mum's life.

JEL. Soph.

ELLIE. I'll owe you. (*She says this next as though it's in air-quotes. Maybe she even does air-quotes.*) 'I'm sorry for calling you a freak.'

SOPH *takes* ELLIE*'s phone.*

How does it work?

SOPH. It's a VPN. You wouldn't understand it.

ELLIE. She unblock yours, too?

JEL. I don't have a phone.

ELLIE. What?

JEL. I don't have a / phone.

ELLIE. Actually what?

JEL. I'm not really allowed on the internet. My mum's worried I'd get cyberbullied.

ELLIE. Right.

JEL. She doesn't like apps. She says teenagers get, like, addicted to technology and it ruins their lives.

ELLIE. I'm addicted to not shitting in a bucket, have toilets ruined my life.

JEL She says they make apps with the same psychology they make slot machines. Like, there was this woman and she was playing *Farmville* and she was so into her game of *Farmville* that when her baby was crying she went like mental and hit the baby's head on the table so she could keep playing *Farmville* and it died.

ELLIE. *Farmville* isn't even that hard, what a loser.

JEL. And she hates selfies. She thinks they encourage the focus of young people's self-worth to be entirely externalised.

SOPH. Your mum took one psychology course and thinks she's Freud.

ELLIE. She's probably just ugly.

SOPH. Done.

SOPH *hands the phone back.*

SOPH. The internet is yours.

ELLIE. Thanks. What are you on, then?

SOPH. What?

ELLIE. You're glued to that thing, what you on all day?

JEL. Oh it's so good.

SOPH. You won't like it.

ELLIE. What is it, porn?

SOPH. No.

ELLIE. Like weird tentacle / porn.

SOPH. No, gross. I just don't think you'd like it.

ELLIE. Why not?

SOPH. Because.

ELLIE. Tell me what it is and I'll decide / if it

JEL. It's a creepypasta board.

ELLIE. A what?

JEL. Like stories and pictures and stuff and they're all creepy.

ELLIE. Right.

SOPH. Shut up.

JEL. What? It's like. It's this big messageboard basically and there's everything and we go on the one for scary stuff.

ELLIE. Scary like how?

JEL. Well, this one time, one of / them was like

SOPH. Jel, shut the fuck up.

JEL. What?

SOPH. She doesn't actually care she just wants / to rip the piss.

ELLIE. Fuck off.

SOPH. There's boards to rate cam-girls, maybe that's more your speed.

ELLIE. Well I'm flattered, but… Come on, try me. Okay. I've seen *Blair Witch*. And not even the remake, the original, and I wasn't even scared. How scary can some shitty chatroom be.

SOPH. Okay.

*She searches on the laptop for a moment.* JEL *watches over her shoulder.*

JEL. Yeah oh my god that one.

SOPH. Okay. So. This one's from a doctor working in the US military on top-secret CIA experiments. They wanted to see what happened if you could make men live without sleep. So. They got these prisoners and they took them to this super-secret high-level security medical facility, way out in the desert. And they made them all inhale this special gas-based stimulant to keep them awake. They stuck them in a hermetically sealed chamber with microphones in the walls and porthole windows for the scientists to look through and make their observations. The first four days everything seemed okay but by the fifth day they were all freaking out. They stopped talking to each other, started whispering to themselves, searching for the microphones in the walls. It was nine days before the screaming started. Just one man first, shrieking and running the length of the enclosure until his throat was so hoarse he could only rattle out his breaths. Then two. Then all of them. Screaming till their vocal cords tore. They ripped the pages from the books they'd been given, smeared them with their shit and stuck them to the windows till the scientists had no way of seeing in, no way of knowing what was going on inside. Then the screaming stopped. The men just went silent. For days and days. They knew they were alive because the oxygen levels were changing, but they were changing crazily, way too much, like the men were breathing double. Eventually they knew they had to go in and check so they made an announcement, like, 'Stand back from the doors, we're coming in. If you comply, one of you will be freed immediately.' But a reply came back from one of the men. 'We no longer want to be freed.' The scientists freaked out, they called armed agents to help them. They drained all of the stimulant gas out of the chamber and opened it up and went in and... One of the subjects was dead. The others...

Their bodies were ravaged. They'd torn hunks of still-living flesh from themselves, their ribcages open and gleaming, their still-working stomachs visible, hanging in their bones, digesting their own flesh as they gorged themselves on themselves. They refused to leave the chamber. 'We will not sleep.' They chanted. One of the soldiers and two of the subjects were killed in the struggle. The final man was pulled, screaming and writhing, from the chamber. The doctors did not understand how he was alive. They took him for surgery but he would not let them put him under, not let them put him to sleep. He begged the doctors for more of the stimulant gas, he screamed and writhed, his heart monitor going crazy, the doctors and soldiers restrained him as he thrashed.

'What are you?!' asked one of the researchers as they tied him down and prepared the anaesthetic.

The guy suddenly goes quiet. He even smiles as best he can with what's left of his face.

'Have you forgotten?' he asks. 'We are you. We are the madness that lurks within you all, begging to be free. We are what you hide from in your beds every night. We are what you sedate into silence and paralysis. We are your animal heart.'

The doctor brings the anaesthetic gas to the man's lips.

'So near.' The man says. 'So nearly free.'

And as soon as he breathes in the gas, his heart stops and he dies.

*Beat.*

ELLIE. Bullshit.

SOPH. There's video.

ELLIE. What?

JEL. I don't like it.

ELLIE. Let's see.

JEL. It's really horrible.

SOPH. You really want to see it?

ELLIE. Yes.

SOPH *plays the Russian Sleep Experiment video.* JEL *watches through her hands. The sound is truly awful. They watch in silence for a good while. Longer than is pleasant.*

So is it true?

SOPH. Maybe.

JEL. I don't think so.

SOPH. CIA stories are kind of lazy cos you can believe they'd do anything. The best ones are family ones or personal stories like family murders / or –

ELLIE. Are any of them true?

SOPH. Yeah. And you can like the story and then the stories with the most likes at the end of the month go on a leaderboard, and you can like comments too and the users with the most likes go on another leaderboard, and it's really significant if someone from a leaderboard weighs in on a discussion of a story, like bollox2bush or catz136, cos they know their stuff.

ELLIE. You on the leaderboard?

SOPH. I don't post.

ELLIE. Why?

SOPH. I just read them.

ELLIE. Why wouldn't you / post?

SOPH. Nothing creepy ever happened to me.

ELLIE. Make something up.

SOPH. It's a hardcore place. If your story isn't good you get trashed in the comments. It's brutal.

ELLIE. Do another one.

SOPH. Alright, kittens in a vacuum or suicide selfies?

ELLIE. Absofuckinglutely.

**3.**

JEL *is crying, shaking, out of breath,* SOPH *calms her,*

SOPH. It's okay, Jel, it's okay. We'll fix it.

ELLIE. What happened to her?

JEL (*quickly, clutching the side of her head*). Nothing.

ELLIE. I heard shouting saw you running.

SOPH. She's fine.

JEL. I hate them.

ELLIE. What happened, Jel?

SOPH. It's none of your business.

JEL. Nicola.

SOPH. Jel.

JEL. They're such dicks it doesn't –

ELLIE. What did she do? Jel, show me.

SOPH. Fucking leave her alone, alright?

ELLIE. Show me.

SOPH. It has fuck-all to do with you.

> JEL *tentatively moves her hands from the side of her head.*
> *There is big wad of bright-pink chewing gum stuck in her*
> *hair.*

JEL. I can't get it out.

SOPH. They're nobodies, Jel, airheads, they're nothing.

JEL. I can't get it out what do I tell my mum?

SOPH. We can cut it out.

JEL. What? Are you actually / out of your mind?

SOPH. I don't think it's that much actual hair in it Jel, / I think
    we can like cut around it.

JEL. Having a big / chunk out of my hair they'll crucify me.

SOPH. We'll be really / careful.

JEL. I'll be so ugly, no.

SOPH. What else you gonna do, leave it? We got maths in five minutes come on.

ELLIE. I can do it if you / want.

SOPH. Stay the fuck out of it, alright?

ELLIE. I cut my own all the time, / I'm good.

*She is taking out her scissors.*

JEL. I don't want to I don't want to I don't want to.

ELLIE. Nicola did this?

SOPH. Who the fuck else?

ELLIE. Where?

JEL. By the big bins.

SOPH. I'll take as little as possible.

JEL. I don't want to.

SOPH. Hold my hand. Look at me. Okay.

SOPH *snips the gum out of* JEL*'s hair*

Okay. It's done.

ELLIE. Give me the scissors.

JEL. Does it look shit?

SOPH *gives* ELLIE *the scissors*. ELLIE *leaves*.

SOPH. Hey those are mine.

JEL. Does it look shit?

SOPH. It looks fine.

JEL. Show me.

SOPH. It looks fine. I hate those sluts.

JEL. Soph shut up and show me, oh my god it's so bristly, it feels so horrible.

SOPH *holds up her phone so* JEL *can see her reflection.*

SOPH. There.

JEL. Oh my god.

SOPH. It'll grow.

JEL. It'll grow? It'll fucking / grow?

SOPH. It's just hair don't be so shallow.

JEL. Don't call me shallow / I'm traumatised.

ELLIE *comes back in, scissors in one hand, the other a clenched fist. They stare at her. She opens her fist and unfurls a severed ponytail.*

ELLIE. Now you're even.

*She throws the scissors onto the floor by* SOPH.

**4.**

SOPH. Girl goes psycho during make-up tutorial?

ELLIE. Even I've seen that one.

SOPH. Deadbaby.com?

ELLIE. What?

SOPH. It's not like how it sounds, its just jokes, you know, why do you put a baby in the blender feet first? So you can see the look on its face. How do you fit a hundred dead babies in a Mini? With a blender. What's the best thing about fucking twenty-two-year-olds? There's twenty of them blah blah. It's kind of boring, they're all reposts.

ELLIE. Right.

SOPH. I feel fantastic?

ELLIE. ?

JEL. It's this creepy sex robot singing a song.

SOPH. A serial killer made her so he could have a girlfriend he wouldn't be tempted to kill.

ELLIE. Go on.

*The video, I Feel Fantastic, plays.*

I love it.

SOPH. Or the cursed toothpaste advert?

ELLIE. No?

SOPH. If you watch it in the daytime or with other people it's just this weird Korean ad for toothpaste but if you watch it alone at midnight there's a demon in it that possesses you.

ELLIE. You ever done it?

SOPH. No.

ELLIE. Why?

SOPH. I don't want to get possessed.

ELLIE. Coward. What's that one?

*She leans over to touch the screen.*

SOPH. Hey.

ELLIE. There. 'The Whistling Woodsman'.

SOPH. It's not got many upvotes, looks a bit shit.

ELLIE. Just read it.

SOPH. Okay. Uh. Last month I went for a walk in the woods near the town I live in. It's really beautiful countryside, thick trees, really untouched. You can walk for hours without seeing another soul. This time of year when the trees are all bare and the leaves are thick orange on the ground it's really eerily beautiful, it's my favourite time to go, by myself, to be with my thoughts. This is dumb.

ELLIE. Shut up, keep going

SOPH. After walking for around an hour I heard something in the distance, like a rhythmic thudding chopping sound. I paused to listen closer. The thudding stopped, but then I heard this sound so creepy my blood froze. It was a whistle. But not like a whistled tune, like a long, high, two-note whistle, more like a hunting call.

SOPH *whistles*.

I spun around to see where the noise was coming from.

And there was a man standing around fifty feet away, in amongst the trees. Really still. Holding an axe. Just standing, staring. He whistled again, this really high-pitched wailing sound

SOPH *whistles*.

And really slowly, like he had all the time in the world, he lifted the axe up onto his shoulder and started to walk towards me, staring straight ahead even though the ground underfoot was all rooted and uneven. He never lowered his eyes once, he just walked, slowly, right for me, staring dead ahead.

And that was enough for me, I ran for it and didn't look back.

At first I didn't tell anyone, I guess I felt embarrassed that I'd got so scared and he was probably just a woodsman or something but then a week later I saw on the news they'd found a body in those woods. Of a young woman. Mutilated. Investigators were still determining cause of death but said it looked like the marks to her body had been made with a heavy blade. Like an axe.

I can't stop thinking about those whistles, and that maybe I made a lucky escape.

*Beat.*

Yeah that one's shit.

ELLIE. I saw him.

JEL. What?

SOPH. Fuck off.

ELLIE. I'm telling / you.

SOPH. That's impossible.

ELLIE. Fuck. The whistles, I heard that, exactly like that, the long two-note whistle. Shit.

JEL. When? Shit, Ellie, you've gone pale.

ELLIE. First weekend we moved here. My dad made me go on a walk in the woods with him. It was super creepy in there, like, really dark in the middle of the afternoon and we got totally lost and then we heard this weird noise and like, at the time I thought it was footsteps but there was no one else around and it didn't really sound like footsteps it sounded much more like –

JEL. An axe.

SOPH. Sure.

ELLIE. I swear on my mum's life. Soph this is really freaky.

JEL. But you didn't see him?

ELLIE. I saw something, like a shadow just like, standing among the trees. And I heard that whistle. And I got cold all over like goosebumps and I asked my dad who the creeper was watching us and he turned and then the guy started walking towards us like, super-slowly through the trees, like it says here, like 'he had all the time in the world'.

JEL. Oh my god.

ELLIE. He didn't look down once to check where he was putting his feet. He didn't pause. He just. Kept coming. And. I ran.

SOPH. He was probably just some wood pervert.

ELLIE. That's what I thought until – (*She gestures to the screen.*) It's exactly the same, Soph. Shit.

SOPH. Bullshit.

ELLIE. I took a photo.

SOPH. Yeah?

JEL. Really?

ELLIE. Yeah. It's on my old phone, I'll bring it tomorrow. I'm telling you. I saw him.

JEL. We should post it.

ELLIE. Hundred / per cent.

SOPH. No.

ELLIE. Why not?

SOPH. This site is like hardcore. Jel's too scared to even have an account.

JEL. No, I just don't sign up for anything cos Mum says hackers can phish you and put your info on the dark web.

SOPH. Christ Jel, nobody on the dark web gives a shit about you unless you're selling nudes and even then you're probably too old for them.

ELLIE. Just post the story, what does it matter?

SOPH. We could get ripped apart in the comments, people on this site are intense.

ELLIE. So what you just shut the fucking thing you don't have to read them, it's not like anyone knows it's you. Just delete the account if it gets nasty. Soph. I saw this guy. For real. We have to let people know he's out there.

SOPH. You'll bring the photo?

ELLIE. Tomorrow.

SOPH. What should I say?

**Interlude**

SOPH. A girl in the forest. A smiling girl on an autumn day in the foliage, dappled light on her face, bare legs stretched, sitting on a log, sticking her perfect pink tongue out and squinting a little in the sun but still beautiful. So beautiful. But something isn't right. Over her shoulder. In the dark of the trees. It could be nothing. It could be a shadow. But look closer. In the shadow beneath a tree, somebody is watching. Staring at the girl. She is caught between him and the camera, unknowing. A stocky, thick figure, dark, his face obscured but over his shoulder, unmistakable now, glinting in the light, the unmistakable outline of an axe.

**5.**

ELLIE*'s bedroom.* ELLIE *is putting make-up on* JEL. SOPH *is on a laptop.*

ELLIE. You have really good skin texture.

JEL. Thanks. You're like a professional.

ELLIE. I used to do pageants.

SOPH. What?

ELLIE. Don't move.

JEL. Really?

ELLIE. Yeah, I was super-good. My dad took me and bought me gowns and paid for tans and everything but he wasn't always allowed in the changing rooms so I had to do my own face which was kind of unfair cos some girls' mums could still help them.

JEL. Why couldn't your mum help you?

ELLIE. This will make your eyebrows look less sad.

SOPH. Isn't that creepy?

ELLIE. What.

SOPH. Pageants.

ELLIE. No? You learn life skills. The teen ones are a bit creepy I guess but I stopped when I was ten.

JEL. Why?

ELLIE. Got boring. I already had a load of trophies so.

JEL. That's amazing

SOPH. I think it's creepy

ELLIE. Good thing no one asked you

SOPH. Telling nine-year-olds their looks are all that matters.

ELLIE. Nine-year-olds already know that. Hold still. You know pretty babies get more attention from adults so they develop better and that's why so many ugly people are introverts. You should let me do you –

SOPH. No, thanks.

ELLIE. You have to make the most of this time. This is the prettiest you'll ever be. The most searched for porn is 'legal teens' so we have maybe three years left before guys start comparing us unfavourably.

JEL. Ellie.

ELLIE. Yep.

JEL. I thought you said your dad had bought a big mansion.

ELLIE. I said he was doing up a big mansion obviously we can't live there till it's done, this is our other house.

JEL. Right. It's nice.

ELLIE. Okay, look up.

JEL. What is that?

ELLIE. An eyelash curler, idiot, hold still.

ELLIE *puts one hand on the top of* JEL*'s skull and with the other clamps the curler around the eyelashes*.

SOPH. Shit.

ELLIE. What?

SOPH. We're in the top ten!

JEL. Really?

SOPH. And another person's spotted him.

ELLIE. Yeah?

SOPH. Yeah. Someone saw him in a forest up in Yorkshire and then. Shit.

JEL. What?

SOPH. Two days later after they saw him this farmer found all of his sheep killed.

ELLIE. Oh my god.

JEL. No! Ow.

ELLIE. Hold still!

SOPH. Their heads totally severed and scattered round the field. Look.

JEL. Poor babies.

ELLIE. Whoa d'you think he cuts all his victims' heads off? Gross.

SOPH. We're on the fucking leaderboard.

JEL. So cool, Soph.

ELLIE. Okay. Now we can take it.

*The girls get in close on the end of the bed for the photo.* ELLIE *holds out the phone at arm's length.*

Not you Soph, hold the light. Okay, look sexy.

JEL. Cheese!

ELLIE. Well, Soph. How do we look?

**6.**

*The girls are sleeping.* SOPH *wakes up. She tosses and turns. She looks about. Something isn't right. She feels under the covers and brings her hand up to her face.*

SOPH. Fuck.

> SOPH *tosses back the covers.*

> Fuck, fuck.

> *She sits up, she peels back the sheet. There is blood on her pyjama bottoms, on the sheet under her, on her hand.*

JEL. Ellie?

SOPH. Sssh.

JEL. What are you – ?

SOPH. Quiet.

JEL. Is that?

SOPH. Quiet.

JEL. Ellie!

ELLIE. What?

JEL. Sophie's sick.

SOPH. I'm not.

JEL. She's bleeding.

ELLIE. Shit my sheets, Soph, Christ.

SOPH. I'm sorry.

JEL. Shall I get your dad? Is she okay? Shall I call / an ambulance.

ELLIE. Are you pigshit? It's her period.

SOPH. I'm sorry.

JEL. Her period?

ELLIE. Why aren't you wearing a pad, it's everywhere.

SOPH. I don't. I don't have any, I've never –

ELLIE. Didn't you bring any?

SOPH. I've never had it before.

ELLIE. Hang on.

SOPH. Don't tell your dad.

ELLIE. I'm not a fucking moron, Soph.

ELLIE *goes*.

JEL. Are you alright?

SOPH. It's still fucking coming.

JEL. Are you alright?

SOPH. This is so gross it won't stop. Oh my god it's all down my leg look why won't it stop.

JEL. It's okay, Soph. Does it hurt?

ELLIE *re-enters*.

ELLIE. Strip the sheet will you? You're getting period all over it.

*She throws* SOPH *a box of tampons*.

SOPH. What's this?

ELLIE. A bag of dicks what's it look like?

SOPH. I can't put one of them –

ELLIE. Why not?

SOPH. That's gross.

ELLIE. You have to plug it.

SOPH. You don't have a pad?

ELLIE. That's all I have.

SOPH. I can't.

JEL. What's the difference?

ELLIE. Tampons go inside.

JEL. Inside?

ELLIE. It's not a big deal.

JEL. Oh my god.

SOPH. I don't want to.

ELLIE. You're getting blood everywhere, Soph, it's disgusting.

JEL. How do you get it in?

ELLIE. Just push it, it's tiny.

SOPH. Oh my god.

JEL. I think we should get your dad.

SOPH *and* ELLIE. No.

ELLIE. Are you kidding? He'll flip. If you get any on my carpet.

SOPH. I'm trying.

ELLIE. Look it's not a big deal, it's tiny, everyone uses them.

SOPH. I don't wanna.

ELLIE. What?

SOPH. I don't wanna touch it.

ELLIE. Touch what?

SOPH. It. My.

ELLIE. Your. Oh my god.

SOPH. It's gross.

JEL. You have to touch it?

ELLIE. If it gets down to the mattress, my dad's gonna freak.

SOPH. Fuck.

ELLIE. Here.

ELLIE *hands* SOPH *a tampon.*

JEL. You can do it, Soph.

SOPH. Fuck.

JEL. I believe in you.

ELLIE. Take it.

SOPH *stands.*

What are you doing you freak.

SOPH. I'm going to the / bathroom.

ELLIE. You'll wake my dad up just do it here.

JEL. We absolutely won't look.

SOPH. How do I –

ELLIE. Just find the hole and push it in.

SOPH. I'm gonna be sick.

ELLIE. It's just a fucking tampon.

SOPH. It's so slippy.

ELLIE *moves towards* SOPH, *goes to put a hand between her legs.*

What are you doing?

ELLIE. I'm helping / you.

SOPH. Gross.

ELLIE. Yeah I'm a lesbian with a period fetish / I'm just

SOPH (*loudly*). Well / don't.

ELLIE. Fuck sssshhh!!

*She puts her hand on* SOPH*'s mouth to shut her up, listens, straining, to the silence. Nothing. Relaxes her hand.*

Look, Soph, look at me. It's fine. Okay?

JEL. Is it finished?

ELLIE. Shut up, Jel.

SOPH. I can't find it.

ELLIE. It's at the bottom. Under the foldy bits.

SOPH. Okay.

ELLIE. Got it?

SOPH. I think so.

ELLIE. Okay, so push. Keep the string on the outside so you can pull it out again.

SOPH. Is it gonna hurt?

ELLIE. I don't know. Just. Do it and see.

SOPH. Okay. Okay.

*She grits her teeth and pushes.*

Oh my god. That's so gross. That's fucking horrible.

ELLIE. Is it in?

SOPH. That's so nasty oh my god.

JEL. Does it hurt?

SOPH. No it's just. It's so nasty.

ELLIE. You did it.

SOPH. Yeah.

ELLIE. Not so bad.

*ELLIE starts to laugh.*

Your face.

SOPH. It's not funny.

ELLIE. You thought I was trying to feel you up, you sicko.

SOPH. It isn't funny!

*Beat.*

ELLIE. You can borrow some pyjamas now, I know you can't bleed on them.

SOPH. Thanks.

ELLIE. Bring a pad next time.

## 7.

*Later that night.* ELLIE *is asleep.*

JEL. Soph? Soph? You okay?

SOPH. Yeah.

JEL. I'm sorry.

SOPH. What for?

JEL. I dunno. Nothing. Does it hurt?

SOPH. No. [*Yes.*]

JEL. I'm kind of. I'm kind of glad I was here.

SOPH. What?

JEL. Like I'm glad I could be here for you when it happened.

SOPH. Okay.

JEL. You know it means you can have babies now?

SOPH. Shut up.

JEL. That's what it / means.

SOPH. Yeah obviously I know, shut up.

   *Beat.*

JEL. Did you know that's what it would be like?

SOPH. I don't know.

JEL. D'you think it's like that every time?

SOPH. I guess.

JEL. For our whole lives?

SOPH. Yeah.

JEL. All this time like teachers and our mums and stuff have been walking round us with that going on and we didn't know. Like everyone's just pretending it's not a thing when objectively it's absolutely bonkers. Like. Father Christmas but backwards.

SOPH (*sitting up*). Stop talking about it. Now.

*Beat.*

JEL. Sorry.

*Pause.*

Do you think we'll ever see him?

SOPH. Who?

JEL. The woodsman that Ellie saw.

SOPH. How should I know?

JEL. I kind of want to? But I'd want you to be there, too.

SOPH. Just. Go to sleep.

**8.**

JEL. Are you coming on the trip, El?

ELLIE. I hate museums they're full of old stuff it makes me dizzy.

SOPH. There's a theory that the whole world is actually a simulation on a computer and if that's true then the past didn't actually exist it was all just like programmed into our collective memory, it never actually happened. And we're all just in this simulation and that's why déjà vu or ghosts or miracles happen, it's just glitches.

ELLIE. So we're all just brains in jars? Bet you'd love that nerd pervert.

SOPH. Absofuckinglutely.

JEL. We can help you fake the signature if you want?

ELLIE. What?

JEL. We can fake your dad's signature on the slip so you can go?

ELLIE (*icy*). Who said my dad wouldn't let me go? I could go if I want to he lets me do anything he doesn't care I just don't want to go to some dumb museum.

JEL. I like it.

ELLIE *looks to* SOPH *and laughs*.

ELLIE. Of course you like it. Nugget?

JEL. Nuggets are meat.

ELLIE. It's a vegetable nugget.

JEL. I know it isn't I saw you buy it.

ELLIE. Don't care.

JEL. You'll get fat.

ELLIE. You sound like my dad. 'Remember all the evil in the whole world happened cos a woman ate something she shouldn't.'

SOPH. Jel only eats sweets.

JEL. Not true.

SOPH. Even at home, like, her mum made us really nice home-
made pizzas at a sleepover once.

JEL. Soph.

SOPH. And Jel went on at her mum about how nice the pizzas
were but then just cut hers up really small and put it in her
pockets and flushed it down the toilet in bits.

JEL. Why would you…?

SOPH. She made the dough and everything.

ELLIE. God, Jel, your mum needs a hobby.

SOPH. That is her hobby.

ELLIE. Go on, have one.

JEL. No.

ELLIE. They're yummy.

JEL. So gross, stop.

ELLIE. Chickens are fucking dumb, it's basically like eating a
carrot.

JEL. The boy chickens are all ground up as soon as they're born
and the girl chickens are kept in these, like, tiny cages so
small they can't / turn round.

ELLIE. Oh my god everyone knows that already.

SOPH. Look, guy in Japan cut off a chicken's head but didn't
sever this one big nerve so the chicken's still alive without a
head and it sort of flaps around in its cage and he feeds it
with a syringe right into its neck hole. You can see right
down it.

*They crowd round the screen,* JEL *a little hesitant.*

ELLIE. What a nutter.

JEL. I think that's terrible and we should find out who he is and he should be / arrested.

ELLIE *suddenly pounces on* JEL, *holding her head and trying to force a chicken nugget into her mouth.*

No get off stop. Soph!

ELLIE. Bcaw! Bcaw! Eat me, Jel, eat me, I'm delicious!

ELLIE *wrestles* JEL *to the ground.*

JEL. Stop it, hey, stop, Soph help!

ELLIE *forces the nugget into* JEL*'s mouth till she can't talk, can't breathe. She coughs and retches, eventually pushing* ELLIE *off. She scrapes the bits of nugget out of her mouth in a panic, coughing and spluttering.*

ELLIE. Oh my god, it was a joke.

JEL. Yeah. I know.

SOPH. Guys! Look.

ELLIE. What?

SOPH. Teen girl missing.

*She hands her phone to* ELLIE.

Right near here. Look, that's the sixth-form college near you, Jel.

JEL. I think I've seen her in the corner shop.

SOPH. She's been missing nearly a week.

ELLIE. You don't think?

SOPH. No. I don't know.

JEL. What?

ELLIE. It could be.

SOPH. I mean. Yeah. I dunno.

JEL. What?

ELLIE. It could be him.

JEL. What?

ELLIE. I mean. Look. She lives right near the woods.

JEL. She probably just like ran away.

ELLIE. Says here she was super-happy, doing well in school, had a Christmas trip planned.

JEL. Right but there was this girl in our sixth form who went missing and it turned out she'd just run to Brighton / with the DT teacher.

ELLIE. I'm telling you, I bet it's him.

SOPH. Fuck.

JEL. Guys.

ELLIE. We should post it.

JEL. Post it?

SOPH. Yeah?

ELLIE. On the site. Do an update. Bet I can find her profile, we can get a better photo.

JEL. But. She's really missing.

ELLIE. Yeah?

JEL. Like. There's a quote from her mum there.

ELLIE. So?

JEL. So, I don't like it. We should go to the police or something / if

ELLIE. Police won't believe us.

JEL. I just really / think we should leave it.

ELLIE. It's not even your account, don't be such a girl.

JEL. Soph?

SOPH. Don't be pigshit, Jel. Let's post it.

**9.**

ELLIE*'s house.* SOPH *and* ELLIE *are huddled around the laptop.* JEL *sits on the bed, bored.*

ELLIE. Look, from a forest guide in California, see the slash marks in the trees?

JEL. Can we do a makeover? Or watch a movie or something?

SOPH. You think it's him?

ELLIE. One of the leaderboard guys does.

SOPH. Just like the slash marks you saw near here.

ELLIE. Where's the map again, where was she last seen?

JEL. Should I get my ears pierced before the dance? Guys?

SOPH. How d'you think he gets around the world so fast?

ELLIE. I have a theory he moves through the roots.

SOPH. Through the roots?

ELLIE. Yeah, like, okay, I know it's super-nerdy but in biology Mr Hobbs said trees can like communicate through this underground root system / and I reckon.

JEL. Guys this is really boring can we play something else?

ELLIE *(icy).* Don't be so rude, Jel, you're a guest.

SOPH. She can't have run.

ELLIE. Nothing was missing.

SOPH. She would just have been in her PE clothes.

ELLIE. It's not like her.

JEL. When's your mansion gonna be finished, then?

ELLIE. Another few weeks, you know what builders are like.

JEL. And then we can go swimming.

ELLIE. Sure.

JEL. Why's your dad here?

ELLIE. What?

JEL. You said he's a pilot so why is he here?

ELLIE. It's his day off.

JEL. Where's he going next?

ELLIE. Africa.

JEL. Africa isn't a country.

ELLIE. Okay then, the People's Democratic Republic of Shut-the-Fuck-Up.

SOPH. There, walking away from the bus stop.

ELLIE. That's totally not far from where I saw him. We entered the woods here.

SOPH. Right.

ELLIE. What do you think he's done with her?

SOPH. I don't know.

ELLIE. Like, cut her head off, like those sheep?

SOPH. And buried her in two different places.

JEL. Guys. I don't like this game any more.

ELLIE. Fuck's sake Jel, stop being a child. There's a TV downstairs go watch CBeebies or something.

ELLIE *and* SOPH *laugh*. JEL *leaves*.

I feel bad.

SOPH. She'll be okay.

ELLIE. I think she hates me.

SOPH. Jel doesn't hate anyone.

ELLIE. I'm not anyone, most people hate me.

SOPH. That's not true.

ELLIE. You hated me.

SOPH. No.

ELLIE. Fucking liar, you / so did.

SOPH. I didn't / hate you.

ELLIE. You absolutely / did.

SOPH. It's actually really narcissistic to think / people hate you.

ELLIE. See!

SOPH. Most people don't actually even think about you as much as you / think they do, so.

ELLIE. Fucking hell talking to you is like trying to plug my charger in the right way up.

*Beat.*

SOPH. I don't hate you now.

ELLIE. Good.

*Beat.*

SOPH. Show me the picture again.

ELLIE *passes* SOPH *her phone.*

I wish we could see his face.

ELLIE. Yeah.

SOPH *swipes on the phone.*

SOPH. Who is that?

ELLIE. My boyfriend. Back home.

SOPH. Seriously?

ELLIE. Yes.

SOPH *makes an inscrutable face.*

What? Bitch, he's nice (*She hits* SOPH, *gently, jokingly.*)

SOPH. Did. Did you really do those things with him?

ELLIE. Yeah. It's not a big deal. You've never had a boyfriend?

SOPH *shrugs*.

It's okay. It's overrated. It was mostly just kissing and him like, foraging around in my pants.

SOPH. Did it feel nice?

ELLIE. Sometimes? I think like… No.

SOPH. What?

ELLIE. I think I kept waiting for it to feel like something more than what it was. But it only ever felt like what it was. Does that make sense?

SOPH. I think so.

ELLIE. He liked to put his fingers in my mouth.

SOPH. What? Why?

ELLIE. Like in a sexy way.

SOPH *makes a face*.

I think it reminds them of cocks.

SOPH. Their own fingers remind them of cocks?

ELLIE. Yeah.

SOPH *splays out her fingers and looks at them*.

SOPH. Like, all the time?

ELLIE *laughs*.

Like tying their shoes? Or playing the piano?

ELLIE. Stop!

SOPH *mimes playing a piano and laughs, imagining ten cocks playing piano*.

SOPH. Finger cocks.

*Her fingers are splayed open. She turns to* ELLIE *and holds up a finger, menacingly.* ELLIE *laughs and half-squirms away and scrunches up her face as* SOPH *places a finger on her temple. They are still, caught between a game and something that is not a game, as* SOPH *traces a line down the side of* ELLIE*'s face very slowly until it comes to rest at the corner of her mouth. She pauses there.*

JEL *enters and they break apart quickly.*

JEL. Guys you have to come see…

JEL *is not entirely sure what she has just seen.*

ELLIE. Fucksake, Jel, you can't just barge in on people, jesus, were you raised by wolves?

JEL. I'm sorry.

SOPH. What the fuck do you want?

JEL. They found her.

SOPH. What?

JEL (*gesturing downstairs*). On the news, they –

ELLIE. What?

JEL. In the woods. They found her… [*body*.]

SOPH. Fuck.

ELLIE *pushes past her and leaves,* SOPH *starts to follow but* JEL *stops her.*

JEL. Soph.

SOPH. What?

JEL. Her stepdad did it.

*Beat.*

SOPH. Her / what?

JEL. It wasn't. He confessed. He'd been… Everyone kind of knew. She was gonna report him so. He. That's what they're saying. It wasn't.

*Pause.*

I'm sorry.

SOPH. It doesn't mean anything.

JEL. What?

SOPH. Just cos this wasn't him. It doesn't mean / anything.

JEL. Soph.

SOPH. He's still there.

JEL. I don't think.

SOPH. We saw him.

JEL. Ellie saw him.

SOPH. She showed us / a photo.

JEL. I think. (*Makes sure she can't be heard.*)

SOPH. What?

JEL. I don't think it was real. I don't think a lot of what she says is real.

SOPH. Why would she lie?

JEL. I don't know, to impress you.

SOPH. Why would she want to impress me?

JEL. Because she likes you.

*Beat.*

I didn't / mean.

SOPH. Fuck you.

JEL. It doesn't matter, Soph.

SOPH. You're jealous.

JEL (*small*). No.

SOPH. You don't want it to be real because it's our thing not yours.

JEL. That's / not fair.

SOPH. Because she's interesting and you're not, because you're scared.

JEL. I'm not scared.

SOPH. Because your fat pigshit mum told you scare stories and like a child you believed them.

*Beat.*

JEL. My mum's a really nice person. And she's just doing her best. I know you wanted it to be real but I don't think it is.

*She moves towards* SOPH, *hand out,* SOPH *knocks it away.* ELLIE *enters.*

I'm not feeling well. I'm gonna call my mum to get me.

ELLIE. Suit yourself. Wait downstairs.

JEL (*to* SOPH, *with an edge*). You two have fun.

*She leaves.*

*Beat.*

SOPH. I can't believe it wasn't him.

## 10.

ELLIE*'s room, later.*

SOPH. She had bits of his skin under her nails from where she'd tried to fight. That's how they got him.

ELLIE. Jesus.

SOPH. Yeah.

*Beat.* ELLIE *looks at her nails.*

ELLIE. I'm sorry.

SOPH. For what?

ELLIE. It's all my fault.

SOPH. / What?

ELLIE. It was my dumb idea to post.

SOPH. I'm glad / we did.

ELLIE. It was stupid, I was so fucking stupid, always so fucking stupid.

SOPH. No, hey, it wasn't. Look. He's still out there, okay? He didn't kill her but. He's out there. You saw him.

ELLIE. Yeah.

SOPH. Other people saw him. I'm glad we did it.

ELLIE. I made Jel hate you.

SOPH. No.

ELLIE. I always do this. I didn't mean to.

SOPH. It doesn't matter, she's being ridiculous.

ELLIE. She's your best friend and I ruined it, I ruined everything.

SOPH. No she's not. I mean. She was. I don't know. I feel like. I don't need her any more. Like. I'm better off without her.

ELLIE. How?

SOPH. So. I think the people around you kind of shape you. And all my life I've been. I've been this one kind of person and maybe I don't have to be, maybe I could be. (*She looks at* ELLIE.) Someone else.

ELLIE *laughs*.

I'm being vulnerable, you dick.

ELLIE. I'm sorry. Just. You don't get a choice.

SOPH. What?

ELLIE. People see you and decide what kind of person you are then they treat you like that person and eventually you just… are that person. So you look like a nerd.

SOPH. I am / a nerd.

ELLIE. Yeah but like do you look like a nerd because you are a nerd or are you a nerd because you look like a nerd? Like if you were pretty people wouldn't treat you like a nerd and maybe you wouldn't have become one.

SOPH. And I'd be a slut like you?

ELLIE. When I was nine and pretty I was one thing. Now I'm thirteen and pretty I'm a different thing. I don't feel like I changed inside. Other people changed first.

SOPH. So you don't have to change inside.

ELLIE. But like. There is no inside.

SOPH. Don't say that.

ELLIE. There is no inside. And even if there is. If nobody sees it, it doesn't matter.

*Pause.*

SOPH. I've been thinking. Maybe we're wrong about him.

ELLIE. I've been thinking that too.

SOPH. What if he's not bad.

ELLIE. Yeah.

SOPH. I found this story, in the Bible. And there was this king, Joshua, and he was tricked by his enemies and instead of killing them as punishment he decided to show them mercy, and so he ordered them to become woodcutters, and to serve the Lord, and it says 'They still serve today.' Maybe he wanted to save her. From her stepdad. And like, when you were there with your dad, he didn't know it was your dad, he just saw a girl on her own with a man in the woods and maybe he just wanted to protect you. Maybe. Maybe he appears so he can help people in danger. Maybe he's there to save us. To save people from death.

ELLIE *thinks about this. She smiles.*

ELLIE. I want to see him.

SOPH. Me too.

ELLIE. I want to know.

SOPH. Me too. How do we do that?

**11.**

*The forest.*

JEL. This is nice. We should have brought a picnic or
something. I only have Skittles. Want some?

*She holds them out to* SOPH.

SOPH. No thanks.

*During this,* JEL *looks up at the treetops. Behind her,* ELLIE
*takes a pair of scissors from her pocket. She passes them to*
SOPH. SOPH *holds them. She stares at* JEL*'s back.*

JEL. I love that smell. When I was little I played this game with
my toys and I plucked loads of leaves off a tree to use in the
game but then I felt so bad cos I knew trees need leaves to
live and I was so worried I'd killed the tree that I went to the
kitchen and got out some Sellotape and stuck all the leaves
back on. I'd totally forgotten autumn was a thing. Isn't that –

*Something happens. A noise? A change of light? The girls all
stiffen.*

Did you hear that?

*They are silent, straining, listening.*

Guys? Did you hear something?

*They listen. The trees rustle. Maybe we hear something.
Maybe it's just the branches. Maybe there's a shadow. Maybe
it's just a trick of the light.* SOPH *raises the scissors.* ELLIE
*looks at her.*

Guys?

*Blackout.*

# SECOND HOME

Charlotte Chimuanya

*For Dad,*
*you've inspired every word.*

*To Mum,*
*you are the star that shines the brightest*
*and leads me to my destiny.*

*Thank you both for allowing me to be free,*
*love you.*

## CHARLOTTE CHIMUANYA

Charlotte Chimuanya trained with National Youth Theatre on the Epic Stages course, and continued her training with a scholarship to study in America on the Shakespeare Academy REP course. She originally performed *Second Home* as a solo show.

Acting credits include *Macbeth* (UK tour); *Hear Me Now* (Tamasha); *Imaam Imraan/Twelfth Night* (National Youth Theatre); *Rockstar* (Lyric Hammersmith) and *Safari/WTTE* (The North Wall).

*Second Home* was first performed at VAULT Festival, London, on 26 February 2020.

*Director*                              Mia Jerome
*Assistant Director*          Tamara Tooher

*At the time of going to print the play was still to be cast.*

Special thanks to VAULT Festival and Nick Hern Books for helping me share this story.

Thanks to the Excellence Festival team and Pleasance Theatre for giving this play its first home and continued support.

Thanks to Titilola Dawudu, Ann Akin, Emma Dennis-Edwards, Belinda Boakye and Somalia Seaton for inspiring and supporting me in my career.

Thanks to Iqbal Khan for encouraging me to share these words.

Thanks to Betusha Rapatusha for being unapologetically free.

Thanks to National Youth Theatre for their training and opportunities that have guided me here.

Thanks to my Irish and Nigerian Family for showing me my roots and my home(s).

And to all of my beautiful, wonderful, creative friends who support me.

*C.C.*

**Characters**

NAOMI, *mixed heritage, aged ten, fifteen and twenty*

*Voices:*
MEAN GIRLS, *Irish accent, female, fifteen*
CLARE, *Irish accent, female, twenty-two*
CONNOR, *Irish accent, male, twenty-four*

**Note on Casting**

The role of Naomi can be played by a single performer or by three actors.

**One**

NAOMI *is ten years old.*

NAOMI. Run, run, come onnnnnn!
   Or the dogs will bite
   Egg-white gnashers
   And a mouth full of parasites

   Quick, with haste, get up this tree
   I saved a spot for you, right here, next to me

   The lush green isle
   With smells of charcoal for two thousand miles
   Granddad winks
   And straight whiskey clinks

   The pubs became… well, not a place to drink
   But a place where we'd watched the sun sink
   Our new playground
   Cobbled streets were our castles

   A gang of royal and rowdy, mucky rascals
   High on banana juice and bags of Skittles
   We were full of tickles and giggles
   Even running through the corridors of hospitals

   Do you remember when you dared me to stick that pencil up
   m'nose? Absolutely class!

   Well, I weren't backing down
   As the new kid on the block
   So I rammed it up there
   And yes… the rubber got stuck

   Rushed to A&E with my mother in a panic
   Every doctor's face read – 'Nigerians Are Manic'

   But it was worth it to join your Wolf Pack
   All of you have blue eyes and mine are jet-black

But that was okay, 'cause I'll learn to adapt
I'll say AYE instead of YES and I'll burn the Union Jack

There I was not a care in the world
Missing two front teeth and head full of curls
Well, they were more like knots
Granny, was never taught how to take care of these locks

*Grabs at hair and looks above to* GRANNY.

Granny, Granny! Just put it under water
She couldn't figure out this foreign texture of her
granddaughter's
But her son, my dad knew just what to do
He'd comb my hair gently and sing a song too

*She sings as* DAD *in an Irish accent – think Irish folk tune:*

　This is your home
　Your second home
　Same time zone
　Different skin tones

　But this, this is your home
　A place where you've grown
　Where you are never alone
　Now this, this is your home

Climbing trees with my cousins
Two boys and one girl
We were rough, used to fight
Chew up oranges and pretend to vomit on sight

I admired the ways they held me up
One quarter of the Wolf Pack
Wild...
And we didn't give a FUCK

Ten years old and I'd just learnt to swear
Only thing different about us was our hair
Hannah's hair fell straight from her crown
Reached wayyy down her back
In the kindest shade of brown

Whereas mine… Defied gravity
And leapt north for all to pree
None of your hair products could ever stop me
She screamed

She yelled and bellowed
Yet I found she did not distract the young fellows
She did not ooze decorum and charm
In fact she scratched and pulled
The opposite of calm

Ten years old and I wasn't bothered
I was yet to see, the ugliness this uncovered

We'd break into closed schools and throw rocks at cars
Mini-troublemakers ready to rebel
Causing havoc and spreading hell

They never told me I was too rough
And not ladylike
Instead they held me up
As their English termite

Ready to chew through society's norms
Break down these walls and the ones who conform

Sometimes we'd approach a rival gang
I'd pretend I understood the trivial slang
Stick out my tongue and we'd run away
Congratulating each other on another successful day

When the sun would set
Beneath the lush mossy hills
We'd retreat to the Wendy house
For horror and thrills

My cousins would aim to scare me the most
Stories about the lonely man next door
And the unfriendly ghost
The guy who bred dogs to kill
And the one who'd slip little girls a sleeping pill

I was beyond terrified
So they stopped all the stories
And fed me pork pies

At the end of that night we all made a pact
If anyone told mums, it was a breach of the contract

*She sings, using her own accent:*

And this is my home
My second home
Same time zone
Different skin tones

And this, this is my home
A place where I have grown
Where I am never alone
Now this, this is my home

## Two

*Lights change.*

*Optional music: 'Now You're Gone' by Basshunter.*

NAOMI *is now fifteen years old.*

*She wears red lipstick, adorns herself in an ill-fitting straight wig and holds a cigarette.*

NAOMI. Back at the playground, older not wiser

This time leaning up against the trees
Our sturdy stabilisers

The park is surrounded by disorderly teens
Hormones racing
Crop tops and baggy jeans

I'm stood by my favourite tree
The one with the most memories

My prettiest cousin Hannah is stood by me
And in front of my eyes all I could see

Was dizzy dinosaurs
Bottles of vodka and nicotine mists
Bums being grabbed and cheeks being kissed

A group of girls are looking my way
Poison in their eyes, rotting like tooth decay

There was a language barrier with how harsh their tongues hit
I could barely make out the distant whispers they spit
But a few of them did stick out in my mind
Wishing my ears to become blind

MEAN GIRLS. Does she speak English?
Why's her hair so stiff?
How dark do you reckon she goes in the sun?

*Beat.*

NAOMI. What should I do?

Should I call them out?
What would I say?
Should I scream and shout?

Ummm, how about:

Does she speak English?
Oh sorry when did you become such a linguist?

Why's her hair so stiff?
Why don't you go jump off that cliff…

How dark do you reckon she goes in the sun?
You know what, come over here for a little one-to-one!

That's exactly what my mum instilled in me
Always hit back twice as hard, but fifteen to one they could literally kill me

So I shut my mouth and keep my head down
Accept that I'll never be queen bee or class clown

In this foreign land I thought all was grand
But I'm starting to feel a little bit too tanned

*Pause.*

Now there's a cute guy coming over to me
He speaks so fast, so liberally
To my surprise he compliments me
Proceeds to put his fag out, on my beloved tree
Then he escorts me and taunts me
Asks me if I'll join him at the beach shortly…

*She nods.*

He held my hand in the car there
Sat in front of me in the passenger
He reached back and searched for my hand
Like a sexy love scavenger

No instructions needed
No directions to my heart
He already had the code
To break me apart…

And break me he did…

Kissing my cousin instead
Like I thought he would
Using me for jealously
Like he knew he could

'Cause I've been searching for love
Ever since I was five
I saw it on the TV
And knew that needed a test drive

*Light-bulb moment.*

Let me tell you a little story about my first love affair.

*Music fades in: the instrumental version of 'Sixpence None the Richer' by Kiss Me.*

I was ten years old
At after-school club

Hanging out by the tyres
With the hottest boy in school

Bleach-blond curtains
Ruby-red lips
He looked like a cross between Leonardo DiCaprio
And that guy from 5ive

We got on to the subject of relationships somehow
And I don't know what came over me
As I was usually the shy one around guys
But the spirit of love took me
And I asked him to be mine

And... he said yes!

I died and shot straight to heaven
I ran away to tell to my bestie, Masie,
And she found the next-best available bachelor on the
playground
And told him – they were now together.
I always loved brazen women.

The next step in this love affair was our first kiss;
Meticulously orchestrated by us bold women.
We met, all four
At the back of the field
Under the romantic pussy willow

Caved in by her bellowing branches, a love nest to seal the
deal.
I remember seeing this kid in Year 1 and understanding the
meaning of love at first sight, and he truly looked happy to
be experiencing this with me.

We all kissed on a countdown, three, two, one GO!
Butterflies? I was feeling fucking doves mate!
The tingles began to spread to places I was yet to explore

Next stop was the dining hall, where he, my love, engraved
'K+R 4 N+M' encased in a love heart onto the dusty window
glass.
In the car he held my hand too as the sun set us our day

A day filled with lust and joy, while moon shone in a silvery-grey.

The next day I woke up smiling
Walked to school and recounted the story
By the time I got there
Everyone knew about last night's glory
I went to put my bookbag away in my tray
And my Romeo met me there to deliver this… cliché

*Beat.*

(*As him.*) You're dumped.

*Music stops – lights up.*

*Pause.*

As the pain and frustration and shame bubbled at the back of my throat;
I couldn't spit out a single word.
I wanted to ask why, but his words had choked me.
I wanted to cry but his rejection had begun a process of self-hate within me.
So I said nothing.

Why was I only treasured as a secret?
Creeping, deep beneath the floorboards
We were sleeping
Am I dreaming?

Then I deeped it:
I guess he didn't want anyone to know that he was with… me
Seems like there was something to be ashamed of, something ugly

Ten years old and I became ashamed
What of?
I was yet to see

*She sings.*

But this is my home
My second home
Same time zone
Different skin tones

But this, this is my home
A place where I have grown
Where I am never alone
And this, this is my home

**Three**

*Lights change.*

*Music fades in: 'Sometimes (Mix #9)' by Erykah Badu.*

*Optional:* NAOMI *rips off her wig, throws it off to the wings and shakes out her afro.*

NAOMI *is now twenty years old.*

*She is clearly happy; she lights up two incense sticks at the front of stage and is enjoying the music.*

NAOMI. At my big age of twenty, I don't know much about Nigeria, but I do know that I FUCKING LOVE the delicate, nuanced flavour that is... Supermalt.

I also know a word from my mother's tongue
Duhum (*Pronounced: 'Do-hoom.'*)
And I was to be surrounded by this word – Duhum
The word of my people,
For the next coming months

*The phone rings. At first* NAOMI *doesn't notice then frantically goes to answer it.*

*Music cuts. Spotlight on* NAOMI.

Hi, Mum, you okay?

…

Yeah my train's booked for six…

…

What…
Uh, uh um okay
Umm, yeah I'll see if I can change it

…

*Pause.*

Mum, is it bad?

…

Okay, I'll be there as soon as I can.

*Music fades in: 'Come Down to Us' by Burial.*

The world really does just carry on around you like nothing
even happened
Like your whole existence didn't just shatter beneath you
It's just like the movies; everything is in fast-forward, whilst
you are stuck on pause
Forever
Forever, a part of you is still

Duhum means Husband
And Didim (*Pronounced: 'Did-im.'*) means Father

*Music fades out.*

They told me to remember to eat, but I was eating
They told me to remember to sleep, but I slept well
Was I doing it wrong?
Three months of sorting bills, they forgot to mention that

They should make bereavement part of the curriculum
Along with mortgages and tax
But they don't want us to thrive, just survive and relax

I didn't know I could cry that much

That my soul could weep for me
When I had nothing left

I didn't know how much I loved you
I wish I knew before you left

I didn't know that, that hug would be our last
But I think that you knew
And I wish I wasn't so rough, so tough
So passive-aggressive towards you
But,
My armour had just began to grow

Death reeks
Yeah man, it's peak
When you need to be strong
But all you feel is weak

That deep, deep dagger
Gliding through your chest
Grief is a physical crucifixion
It's a test

A test that no one can fail
As we must prevail
Keep your sanity protected, behind this veil

Don't let them see you fall outside of these walls
Just stick on a smile and stand up tall

It's been three days since I saw you in that hearse
Fourteen since I hugged that practical nurse

The one who seemed way too young
Wise beyond her years
She'd already tackled those unspoken fears

When you suffer from grief within the early stages
You care more about connections, and less about wages

Your angle of reflection becomes immediate correction
Our girls in blue, skin thicker than Granny's Irish stew

*Beat.*

Ten Hail Marys and we sent you on your way
But death reeks and stayed with me for three days

In and out of churches to give thanks and praise
We buried you in your hometown so why the hate

Hannah told me last night…
At the piss-up in the castle
Wow, the whispers the lies and the theories unravelled
Before my eyes a detachment took place
Half of me frazzled before my face
A part of me died last night along with you
The innocent little girl who had no clue

About this cruel world and its inhabitants
Including my family? FUCK!! Need a psychoanalysis

What did Yolanda call it? A quarter-life crisis
The right to love should come with a licence
An authority to tell you when you're doing it wrong
When you've really fucked up, you can't just string me along

Twenty years too late and I learned the truth
With their fake smiles showing every tooth

Yes
Death reeks
But it turns out – my Irish family's racist views were hardest
to conceal??!

Twenty years of bliss, the ignorant kind
I feel so stupid to have been so blind

Apparently, when you first introduced your exotic bride
The family were gobsmacked, hurt by their pride
I would have loved to see their faces, when you opened the
door
I'm sure, all jaws, swiftly hit the floor
And the village felt a rumble from the roars at 214
What a rebel, my mother was
Dark skin, pregnant and lost in the middle of Oz

I heard Granny cried when she heard I was coming

'Not a (*Whispers.*) black child!?'

She thought you were bluffing

*Pause.*

I guess you were brave to bring me into this world
Maybe thought you'd bring change with your black baby girl
Maybe bring an exchange, a mind rearranged
And maybe you did but what happened was so strange

One granny
One granddad
One mother
Two aunts
Three uncles
And a doctor, smiling with eyes hollowed
Walked up to this room, each of us followed
Crammed into this space to meet our grace
'There's nothing more we can do,' he explained with pace
The cancer has spread
From his toes to his head
Machines are breathing
Your choice is next
In the ICU
Do you see me
Did you see that, Mum
A tear
Fell so softly
After I read him that poem
Just wanted to show him
That I was so strong
And all was forgiven
And when I saw that tear
Roll down your face
I knew it was due to the words that I had written
I gave you a piece of my soul in that moment
To take up with you, from me a bestowment

Goodbye, now forever
Your eternal warmth turns to frozen and pale

Have you ever smelt green
Keep it somewhere safe
Synesthesia, 2:1
Cut his hair
You were so proud
Happy birthday, today, fifty-one
Guilt, so much guilt
Twenty-five years of marriage
Tie it in a ribbon
And anger starts to rear
Hate hate hate
Anger hate
FEAR

*She sings:*

> But this was my home
> My second home
> Same time zone
> Different skin tones
>
> And this, this was my home
> A place where I had grown
> Where I was never alone
> Now where, where is my home...

*Lighting should indicate a change of location.*

I'm back in the place where I came of age
But everything's different, dull and grey
The playground is gone, and the trees
Instead stand new houses – several of these

I have no energy left to cry
Just leave me here to crumble and die
Before I could even drop to my knees
I feel a tug on my dress and I turn around to see...

Well, to my surprise
My eye gaze drops to three-foot-five
She looks about four
Sweetness to the core

She is mixed race with
Rosy cheeks on her face
Hair tied up in those familiar knots
And eyes that shine bright at two thousand watts

Is this an angel come to set me free?

*Beat.*

Then I hear her mother screaming, ROSIE, ROSIEEEEE!

There's a woman running towards me, her name is Clare
She's got freckly white skin and flame-filled hair
She looks powerful and strong
About my age, but, she's already a mum

CLARE. Oh hello there
    Rosie come here
    Sorry about that love

NAOMI. Hi

    I reluctantly said

CLARE. Aren't you that wee McCarthy girl?

NAOMI. I nodded with dread

    I go to leave, wipe my tears on my sleeve
    then something changed, something happened to me

CLARE. Hey, wait have you been crying, what's wrong, love…

    Ah you buried your daddy just then didn't you, I'm so sorry
    Do you wanna come in for a cup of tea.

NAOMI. Oh, no thank you. I better get home.

CLARE. No, you can't go home like that, you're wet,
    You've been crying and well I won't have it.
    Come on in,
    The fire's going and
    The kettle's just boiled
    And I could do with some company

    *Beat.*

Plus, Rosie would love to meet you, she looks smitten.

NAOMI (*laughs*). She's cute.

CLARE. Aye, well she's got her daddy to thank for that, God help her when those freckles come through, she'll be batting them off at school.

Now come on in would you, I've gotta start tea for her daddy. It's toasty and warm in there; come and have a cup of tea will you not?

*Beat.*

Go on, I'll add a bit whiskey in it for ya, make it really Irish

NAOMI (*laughs*). Go on then

CLARE. Ah good girl, come on Rosie, come and meet... ah what's your name there, lass?

NAOMI. It's Naomi.

*Optional:* NAOMI *sits on the chair; she wraps a blanket around herself and holds the mug.*

*Lighting should reflect a cozy fire, a relaxed environment, crackling fire sounds and a TV in the background.*

I love this show, I began to tell her
The one with the detective and the saboteur
Little Rosie stared up at me
I couldn't help but be a bit – awkwardly

I wondered if she'd ever seen a truer reflection
Than the one in the mirror we see
Not many of 'us' around here
Please, baby girl, keep that smile from ear to ear
Don't let anyone tell you, you're ugly 'cause you're different
Ignore their harsh, critical belligerence
Keep your chin high with that crown on your head
In fact let me help you – maybe braids or even dreads.

I ask her mum if I could be of assistance
She gives in, taking the path of least resistance

Rosie calmly sits between my knees
I explain, beauty is pain and break out the grease

*Optional:* NAOMI *takes grease from the prop area and
applies a generous amount to her left hand ready to do
Rosie's hair in front of her – starts braiding.*

I started to tell little Rosie
About her new home
Built on top of my playground
Now covered in brick and chrome

How we'd climb trees and throw rocks but she should never
be so naughty
How I'd visit her and her mum and fix her hair if it was too
knotty

*We hear a text message notification come in –* NAOMI *looks
concerned.*

Can I use your loo?

CONNOR. Hey Ni,
Hannah went way too far last night
We were all wasted but I could feel your heart breaking
I'm not gonna deny, that what she told you was true
But she had no right to cut you that deeply

Aye Granny and them have their theories, their wee
gossiping
But they're stuck in the past
You know that, come on now
We're not all like that I promise
And I want you to know
You're still loved
You and your mum
My aunt
My family

Hey look, do you think it was easy me coming out to them
Fuck no!
They've never looked at me the same
But we are the next generation

We can't choose how we are treated
But we can choose how to treat others...

Fuck me... that was a tad profound, weren't it?

I wish we were still climbing trees
And breaking into buildings
Remember when I dared you to stick that pencil up your nose?
Absolutely class!

Hey Ni, you listening?
You know us McCarthys, we only get soppy six whiskies deep
We're made of tougher stuff than this
But I'm here for you if you need to talk
In fact come over now if you want, I've got half a bottle of Buckfast
And a couple ciggies with your name on 'em
Listen to me now – your daddy wouldn't want you to cry
You are Irish!
Whether they like it or not
So come on over, let's drink to that!

NAOMI. And yeah, he's right
I am Irish! And this *is* my home!

I don't look it, I don't look much Nigerian either
Yet, somehow, I am both, and I'm proud of that.

I think I'm ready to face the world again
Ready to learn more about who I am
Still hurting, but stronger.

*Music fades in: 'Stronger' by Sugababes.*

*End.*

# MADAME OVARY

Rosa Hesmondhalgh

*For Rumii and AC/DC*

## ROSA HESMONDHALGH

Rosa Hesmondhalgh is a writer and actor from Yorkshire. Shortly after graduating from LAMDA in 2017 she was diagnosed with ovarian cancer. During treatment, she started a blog from her hospital bed called *Madame Ovary*, that she started to turn into a one-woman play after she went into remission. *Madame Ovary* was first performed at the Pleasance, Edinburgh, in 2019, where she won the VAULT Pick of the Pleasance Award. *Madame Ovary* is touring the UK in 2020.

*Madame Ovary* was first performed at the Pleasance as part of the Edinburgh Festival Fringe, on 31 July 2019. The cast was as follows:

| | |
|---|---|
| ROSA | Rosa Hesmondhalgh |
| DOCTOR NO BULLSHIT | Lesley Molony |
| *Director* | Adam Small |
| *Movement Director* | Rebecca Stanier |
| *Lighting Designer* | Holly Ellis |
| *Producer* | WildChild Productions |

This play is about a life being saved, and the people who saved my life were NHS doctors, nurses, technicians, porters, health-care assistants, pharmacists and psychologists. Thank you, thank you, thank you. I will fight for our brilliant health-care system as it fought for me! x

Huge thanks to Adam Small, Lesley Molony, Rebecca Stanier and Holly Ellis for their incredible help in bringing this story to life. Thanks to Eva Scott, Joe Aldous, Julie Hesmondhalgh, Ian Kershaw, Shelly Silas, Marissa Ogbeide and Zoe Alker for reading early drafts and soothing my panicky phone calls. Thanks to Hessies, Stewards and Bye Bye Little Sebastian for coming to visit me in hospital and then coming to see me in Edinburgh. Thanks to all the team at Trekstock, Ovarian Cancer Action, CLIC Sargent and Macmillan. And loads of love to the Badass Babes, all of whom have kicked, or are kicking, cancer's arse.

*R.H.*

**Characters**

ROSA

DOCTOR NO BULLSHIT
PANEL MEMBER
NURSE
SURGEON
TECHNICIAN
JESS
LIZZIE
UBER DRIVER
BRIDGET
LOUIS THEROUX

**Note on Play**

Every character, other than Rosa, can be brought to life by a
mixture of voice recordings, projections, or the actor playing
the parts.

**Note on Staging**

There is a projector screen onstage.

ROSA *is jogging on the spot.*

ROSA. This. Is my year.

*The words '2018 RESOLUTIONS' flash onto the screen.*

This is the year I sort my shit out and become the person I have always known I could be.

*The first resolution: 'I WILL GET MY PRIORITIES RIGHT' appears on the screen.*

Passionate, dedicated, hardworking. Fully recognising my worth. Not responding to 3 a.m. 'you up' texts. Not composing 3 a.m. 'you up' texts. Work hard, call my grandma, spend time with my friends. And –

*'I WILL TAKE BETTER CARE OF MY BODY' appears on the screen.*

That means drink more water, drink less alcohol, exercise regularly.

Towards the end of last year, I gained a bit of weight. You know, it's classic Christmas weight.

Mince pies and mulled wine. I'm just noticing I've got a bit of a stomach on me, and I want to tone up a bit. Nothing drastic. Just so I can see my Christmas pedicure when I look down in the shower.

SO, I've started jogging on the spot whilst watching TV.

I am planning on giving up alcohol for a whole month – just not this month, because I've got a Tinder date on Friday and I don't want to be sober for that.

*A video of a yoga instructor appears on the screen.*

And I've started one of those month-long yoga plans. You know, the ones where no one can get past day seven.

*She gets into position.*

I'm up to day fifteen.

*The video plays for a few seconds,* ROSA *follows along. Suddenly –*

Ow. Feels like I've been overdoing it. Maybe those abs I'm after are growing. No sign of them yet.

But pain is good. I've read that that means muscles are breaking and growing back in a more Instagram-worthy fashion. One thing I've learnt about being a woman, is pain is usually an indicator of good things coming. Right?

*The third and final resolution: 'I WILL MAKE SOME REALLY GOOD ART' appears on the screen.*

Since graduating drama school, the phone hasn't exactly been ringing off the hook with auditions.

I know that to shut out the little voice that tells me I've wasted twenty-seven grand plus maintenance on an Arts Degree, I have to MAKE my OWN art, and it has to be REALLY GOOD.

Something no one has seen before. Something fucking sick. Something that will make people go, 'ooh', but also, 'ohhhh'.

I've been writing poetry since secondary school where the heartbreak of not being cast in *Othello* inspired me to write 'I Want to Be Iago Moor than Aidan Braithwaite Does'.

*The title appears on the screen.*

*Almost immediately, a Tinder notification pops up on the same screen.* ROSA *clicks on it and reads it. It says something like, 'How about this pub? It's halfway between us both.'*

I met a long-term boyfriend on Tinder, so don't knock it. We were together for two-and-a-half years. He was generally great, he just asked me to choose between him and acting quite a lot. In the end I wasn't really choosing, because some of the best acting I've done was pretending I was still interested in him.

*Resolution Number One: 'I WILL GET MY PRIORITIES RIGHT' pings onto the screen. ROSA impatiently swipes it away and replies to the message.*

I've been single for about four months, depending on who you ask. If you ask the last guy I was dating he'd tell you I've been single a lot longer than that, because we weren't actually in an exclusive relationship, we were more of a fluid meeting-of-minds. Who were allowed to sleep with whoever else he wanted. And I was happy with the fluid meeting-of-minds thing. Really happy. I mean I'd never heard the term coined like that, but he would sometimes leave crystals and wind chimes around my bedroom so I knew we had something special. I think it was a matter of just waiting until we were ready. Until we were ready to commit fully to each other. Until we were prepared to stop playing the field and just, you know. BE. With each other. Until we were in a place where we weren't actually a free spirit who rides on the winds of chance and runs away from the bindings of romantic commitment and can't actually give something that could be really good just a bit of a fucking chance. But yeah in the end I just think we might have wanted different things, so we went our separate ways and we're planning to meet up for coffee as friends at some point when he's less busy.

*She goes back onto Tinder and swipes through a few dead-looking options.*

Most people on these apps scare the shit out of me because I know they're the type of boys who would have thrown my tampons around maths in secondary school, but have grown up into insurance salesman who live in Earl's Court.

There was one guy whose opening line was 'What's your IQ?' Which is nearly as gross as another one that said, 'How many people have you slept with then?' And actually the answer is the exact same number for both.

But this guy seems. Nice.

*She rubs her stomach absently.*

*RESOLUTION NUMBER THREE APPEARS ON THE
SCREEN ALMOST AGGRESSIVELY.*

Twenty-three, F.
Long red hair.
Peeling the layers of my skin back to see what's hidden
there.
Don't know what I should be yet
Nor do I know where.
Feels like playing life is hard and the rules are unfair.
Wish I could be more like those girls on the internet.
You know who you are and you have a voice there
Twenty thousand followers across your social media
You're online all the time yet I come across a lot needier
The height of your standards is incredibly admirable
And the light of your enlightenment as bright as a candle
I follow you miles past your Twitter handle
My DMs left forgotten like a jelly sandal
Story of my life
Popular with kids
Quirky in 2011
Not really seen outdoors after half past seven oh for fuck's
sake no that's shit.

*Lights normalise.*

It's all shit.

I feel a bit shit.

Even if I could finish something, write a poem that's talking
about something important, or a short story or a play that
meant something to people... I don't think I could deal with
anyone's criticism.

Any one-woman show I write will be compared to *Fleabag*.
And what would it be about? Lying on the floor with a
stomach ache? The portrait of the artist as a whiny bloated
woman who can't get an acting job?

And actually I'm really struggling to know what story I want
to tell, but I know I need to tell it.

It's so important to tell your story.

Because otherwise people will keep asking you, 'So what you doing next? You write, don't you? Are you working on anything at the moment???'

And if you call yourself a writer, and don't write, people will write you off, and then write the story for you. So I need to get cracking. For other people. Because I've always been good at this, acting, writing. So people are expecting it of me. So I should get on with it.

Fuck. I do think I might have IBS though.

*'I WILL TAKE BETTER CARE OF MY BODY' flashes up on the screen.*

*'Pretty Ugly' by Tierra Whack plays.* ROSA *moves through her daily life, constantly distracted by pain and her stomach. The song ends abruptly.*

It's Friday morning and my Tinder date is tonight. Problem is, my jeans and nice top won't fit over my stomach. I've avoided gluten all day, I've even eaten a fucking Activia yogurt to try and combat the bloating, but it actually seems to be getting worse.

Luckily I have some black, billowy, stretchy trousers – a purchase made whilst trying to impress the crystals-and-wind-chimes boy.

*She observes herself in the mirror. Resolution Number Two appears on the screen. She swipes it away immediately.*

I'm afraid there is absolutely no way I am having sex with Tinder Boy. I keep having visions of taking my clothes off and having to explain to him why I look like a less 'break the internet' version of Beyoncé's pregnancy photos.

'Yeah, I know what it looks like, but don't worry, I think it's actually just a massive poo in there.'

I think I'll do myself more favours if I just pretend I'm a put-out-on-the-second-date kind of girl and keep my bump covered.

And the date is brilliant.

Tinder Boy is brilliant. He is funny, down to earth and had an absolutely horrific time at secondary school which means he doesn't care in the slightest about seeming cool. He's intelligent, likes reading and we have the exact same music taste. We've both seen every single Louis Theroux documentary, which probably isn't high up on the list of most people's specifications for their ideal partner, but it is for me. I've been watching his documentaries since I started my A levels, and I'd break up revising with *Weird Weekends*. At first I was just fascinated by the topics he covered, but then I started to just love the way he handled everything.

He just balances kindness with bluntness, humanity with humour, he studies the outskirts without skirting round the issues there, he's also a bit weird, like the episode where he –

*Something changes in* ROSA *but it's not entirely clear.*

Do you want another drink?

This is really weird, my leg's gone numb. Like completely numb. From what? The four rum and Cokes I've drunk? Have I been stood in a weird position as we've leant against this table in the pub? Is it my terrible yoga technique? Or is it my body having an adverse reaction to meeting a brilliant man on a dating app and going into cardiac arrest at the unlikeliness of it all?

*She swipes away the resolution again.*

I don't tell Tinder Boy that my thigh has suddenly lost its sensation, because I'm a bit worried he might try and cut our date short and take me to the hospital or something. I'm half-waiting for the numbness to spread all over my body and cause me to collapse – but it doesn't. The pub closes, and he walks me home. There's this expectation lingering between us as we hover outside my front door. I don't invite him in, obviously – but not just because of my quite literally cock-blocking midriff, but because. I quite like him. And I don't want to rush into anything. Which is a first.

*Sudden pain, we've moved forward in time.*

I swear to God, I'm never doing fucking yoga again. The next morning, my back and ribs start to ache. Everything hurts. A weird trapped nerve in my leg, a distended stomach, a bad back. Why am I falling apart?

*Resolution Three appears.*

I have an audition for a big poetry slam this weekend, and a full day of work.

Every time I eat, my stomach grows to the watermelon shape I've been getting used to, and my back aches more. I am too busy to be this constipated.

*The lights change. We are at a poetry reading.*

> I won't eat anything with a face
> So clocks are off the menu
> Time
> And time again
> You pretended you were vegetarian and then you
> Slept with me.

PANEL MEMBER. Is that it?

*The* PANEL MEMBER *is wearing sunglasses inside.*

ROSA. Yes.

PANEL MEMBER. It's a very short poem.

ROSA. Well, it's indicative of the length of the relationship the poem's about.

PANEL MEMBER. Thanks for coming in.

ROSA. Even the disgruntled blow to my poetry-writing skills isn't enough to deflate my stomach back to a normal size.

I drink peppermint tea and lie in bed.

*She swipes away Resolution Two and a couple of messages appear, from friends with bloat-reducing tips like: 'are you drinking peppermint tea?', 'you should try buscopan', 'lol*

*how are you gonna live without bread m8', and then one
from Tinder Boy, referring to their date.*

*She falls asleep.*

*The time reads 4.37 a.m..*

I am wide awake from pain. Every position I try to shift to, it
gets more difficult to breathe.

*Resolution Two appears.*

If I go to A&E, they'll probably laugh at me for turning up in
the dark with a stomach full of farts.

But at least I might be able to take my clothes off in front of
Tinder Boy tomorrow.

*To A&E.*

Hi. Um. I think I have trapped wind?

The nurse takes me through to a cubicle with a curtain pulled
across.

NURSE. When did the pain start?

ROSA. About a week ago.

NURSE. And the bloating?

ROSA. Just less than a week ago.

NURSE. Any change in your bowel habits?

ROSA. Erm. A bit. But that might be because I've not been able
to eat, really.

NURSE. Why?

ROSA. Because every time I do, my stomach gets bigger, and
the pain gets worse.

NURSE. Are you sexually active?

ROSA. I hate that question. I've always been too proud to ask
what it actually means. Does it mean have I had sex EVER?
And when I first did it, I activated a setting that updated me
into a sexually active person?

Or does it mean, am I actively having sex? Every day? Every week? That sex is an activity that I partake in regularly, like. I don't know. Tennis.

ROSA. Yes, I am.

NURSE. Alright –

ROSA. I've not played tennis since I was in Year 7.

NURSE. Is there any chance you could be pregnant?

ROSA. I've had sex since then though.

   (*To* NURSE.) No, there isn't.

NURSE. Do you have a regular partner?

ROSA. Not that I had sex when I was in Year 7.

   (*To* NURSE.) No, I don't.

NURSE. We'll take some blood, and do a pregnancy test, just in case.

ROSA. Then I have to lie on my back and she feels my belly. She takes two fingers and places her hand on top of them, and taps. She taps above my belly button, below, and then rolls me over to my side and taps there too. The sound changes.

   She looks down at me and says.

NURSE. I think you're full of gas.

ROSA. I look up at her and say, 'I've been told that my entire life.'

   *Resolution Number One comes up.*

   *She acknowledges it, records a voice note to her family.*

   Hi, guys, I know you probably thought if one of your kids would be calling you from A&E it'd be Joe – my brother's just gone on his gap year – but I've been having some weird stomach pain. Nothing to worry about, they think it's trapped wind – will keep you posted. Love you.

I am called back in.

NURSE. Your bloods have all come back normal, except a little abnormality in your liver profile.

ROSA. Oh. That could be this special brew my flatmate once made me drink.

NURSE. I've paged a doctor to come and see you. You can – you can stay here where it's quiet. I'll get you some pain relief.

ROSA. She smiles and draws the curtain across.

*Checks phone, 8.30 a.m..*

*Resolution Three flashes up. She swipes it away.*

That'll have to wait.

*Tinder Boy messages. She swipes it away.*

So will that.

SURGEON. Knock knock.

ROSA. Two surgeons enter from behind a curtain, which incidentally cannot be knocked on. They start to tap on my stomach again. Above the belly button. Below. To the side. The sound changes. They straighten up.

SURGEON. It might be worth getting you an ultrasound, Rosa. Hard to tell anything without having a proper look.

ROSA. Okay.

*A message from Tinder Boy appears.*

I need to be somewhere by 8 p.m..

I am sent to ambulatory care, which is like A&E but smaller, louder, and full of people who have all been told they'll be seen at 9 a.m.. I hope I'll be seen quickly, then sent home with armfuls of laxatives so I can head home and shave my body hair before my date.

To ultrasound.

TECHNICIAN. This'll be cold.

*An ultrasound appears on the screen. ROSA watches.*

You seem to have a lot of fluid around your organs.

ROSA. Not gas? I was told it was gas.

TECHNICIAN. It's definitely not gas. You see all this black stuff on the screen? That's fluid. It shouldn't be there.

ROSA. For some reason all I can see is a baby. Its head. Its little feet.

TECHNICIAN. This is your liver. Your bowels. Did you know you have a kidney in your pelvis, rather than your back?

ROSA. Yeah. I did, actually. I had kidney stones as a teenager, and they found the weird kidney then.

TECHNICIAN. That's quite rare. But the fluid is surrounding most of your organs. So we should book you in for a CT scan.

*The time appears. It's 11 a.m..*

It's okay. I'll make sure you're seen quickly.

ROSA. I go back out to the packed-out waiting room.There are no seats, but a man stands up and offers me his. The woman next to me beams. She asks me when I'm due.

*The time, 2 p.m., appears on the screen.*

On to the CT scan. I have to be nil-by-mouth, which is fine because I haven't eaten since yesterday. My stomach rumbles as I roll back and forth in the tube.

*More X-ray-type pictures appear on the screen.*

The results will be ready in an hour.

*Resolution Two appears on the screen.*

That seems like enough time to go and get some food and a cup of tea from the hospital café but as soon as I return the nurse on reception tells me the surgeons are looking for me.

That was fast.

I've only been gone ten minutes. I've not even had time to finish my porridge.

I'm told to wait in a side room on the bed.

I text my family, my friends and Tinder Boy to update them.

They've found something weird in my liver.

A surgeon comes through the door,
Behind him two more
And it seems a little excessive
to deliver the message
from one CT scan.
They sit down and the energy drops with them
So I do what I can
To lighten the mood
welcome, lads, I say, to my humble abode
Don't worry about your shoes.
The most senior surgeon speaks.

They've found *something weird* in my stomach.

The fluid all around my organs
That they've confirmed in the scan
Is what's causing all the bloating and they're hoping to take
a sample to test
They search my face to check if I'm listening
And I am
But I'm also wondering if there's a chart that exists
That tells you exactly what all the different colours of scrubs
mean.

They've found *something weird* in my left side.

Not gas. A large mass.
Around fifteen centimetres across.
It's down near my pelvis.
It's got its own blood supply.
That's probably just my weird kidney.
I say. And eat a spoonful of porridge.

No, we've noticed that and whilst that is a rarity,
We need to do some further scans to see what it could be.
You're very young though. You're very healthy.
'It'll be fine then?' It should be.
Just need to rule out some things.
One of the other surgeons takes the sample of fluid.
He is really good looking.

I warn him I smell of porridge.
He warns me this might hurt a bit.

He draws *something weird* out of my stomach.
That's the fluid?
I'm surprised at the inky black of it.
It's very bloodstained. He says.
But I don't know what he means by that.
I don't know what he's getting at.

I'm sent out to the waiting room again.
Pull my phone out, it's about 6 p.m..
I open my messages and sigh.
'They're keeping me for longer, I won't be out by eight.'
He'll understand, he's such a nice guy.
I hope he doesn't think I'm trying to get out of the date.
Do I put a kiss?
I've been here for ten hours,
It's starting to feel
Like there's *something weird* about this.

Internal ultrasound.

So instead of jelly on a stick that goes: (*She demonstrates.*)

It's jelly on a stick that goes: (*She demonstrates.*)

This is the most action I've had in months.

I don't think he gets it.

There's a female doctor next to him, to chaperone. She tells
me her name's Jess and she keeps me chatting and distracted
whilst the contents of my womb are examined.

She asks me if I'm okay.

I'm fine. Just a bit tired now. It's been twelve hours.

JESS. Okay, Rosa, I'm just going to give you a bit of tissue to wipe everything up, and then if you just pop your trousers back on and I think the head of gynae wants to come and speak to you.

ROSA. It's not exactly being told the head of casting at the National wants to speak to you, but I still feel a bit important.

She is one of the most no-bullshit women I've ever met.

DOCTOR NO BULLSIIIT. We've found the mass. Along with several other abnormal growths in your lymph nodes, stomach lining and omentum.

*Long, long pause.*

ROSA. What the fuck is an omentum?

DOCTOR NO BULLSHIT. We need to do an MRI scan to figure out how abnormal.

ROSA. How do I have organs in my body that I didn't know existed?????

DOCTOR NO BULLSHIT. So we'll send you back down to A&E to wait for a bed and then we'll get you an MRI first thing in the morning.

ROSA. Is the omentum even an organ? Where is it? Why do I have one and WHY HAS NO ONE EVER TOLD ME ABOUT IT????

Jess takes me down to A&E and it is heaving.

There are trolleys from ambulances queuing up and there must be fifty people lined up along the walls on overflow plastic seats. There are no chairs for me. There are a few beds, that are filled with people, although it seems completely pointless, as there's no possibility of sleep because of the sensory overload. The sounds, the bright light, the smell. I'm brought another plastic chair from the staffroom and given a hefty dose of pain relief. I put my headphones in and start the episode of Louis Theroux's *Weird Weekends* where he goes to Broadway, and I've not even got to the part where he sings George Michael when my flatmate Lizzie explodes into A&E.

LIZZIE. They wouldn't let me bring the flowers in. They're at the desk. That's a weird rule, don't you think – oh my God look at all this. You're not getting a bed here. Not a chance. Not until 6 a.m.. You've been here for hours. We only live round the corner, you need a proper rest. A bath.

ROSA. Lizzie disappears into the masses and when she returns, she picks up my bag.

Are we going home?

LIZZIE. Yep, you're to be back at the maternity ward tomorrow, first thing. I'll get us an Uber.

*The Uber.*

UBER DRIVER. Where've you ladies been tonight?

ROSA. Um. The hospital.

UBER DRIVER. Oh. Everything okay?

ROSA. Yes. Well. I don't know. They found a mass in my stomach apparently. It's been hurting loads for about two weeks.

UBER DRIVER. Don't worry. That'll be nothing. That'll be nothing, my girlfriend, right, she had a tumour in her brain, right, and she couldn't feel anything. So if you're in pain, it's nothing to worry about. Nothing at all.

*Silence.*

ROSA. Is your girlfriend alright?

UBER DRIVER. Who? Oh yeah, she's great.

ROSA. The MRI is long. It's loud. It's painful.

*We hear the sound of the MRI.*

Jess takes me back to the maternity ward to wait for the results, and then quickly finds me a side room after the third expectant mother asks my stomach about baby names.

*The time, 1 p.m., flashes up on the screen.*

A nurse I've never seen before knocks on the door. She knows my name.

NURSE. We've got the results of your MRI, Rosa. Is… is someone coming to join you at any point today?

ROSA. My mum. She's getting the train down. She should be here in the next hour.

NURSE. Okay. Okay. Well, we might wait until then. Sometimes it's good to just have an extra pair of ears, just so you're hearing all the correct information.

ROSA. She leaves the side room. I lie back on my bed and press play on the episode of *The End of the Fucking World* I am watching.

I have cancer. Don't I?

Thirty-four young adults are diagnosed with cancer every day. My day is 1 February 2018.

DOCTOR NO BULLSHIT. Think of it as a sort of apron.

ROSA. It's about 6 p.m..

DOCTOR NO BULLSHIT. It hangs down from our stomachs and liver and covers and protects our organs.

ROSA. I've got cancer.

DOCTOR NO BULLSHIT. It doesn't have a vital function, which is why not many people have heard of it.

ROSA. But at least I know what an omentum is.

DOCTOR NO BULLSHIT. I can confirm it's not epithelial.

ROSA. I don't know what this means.

*Words like epithelial, germ cell, can't be treated here, radiotherapy, removal of ovaries, painkillers, drain the*

*ascites, options, biopsy, we need to investigate further, are*
*either on the screen or said out loud or both.*

I don't know what this means. I don't know what any of this
means.

There is just this beeping
It's in keeping with the blocked signals in my head
So I have to check when I leave the room that it's external
I'm being taken to A&E to wait for a bed
But the beeping is fucking infernal
I can't even remember the details of what's been said

I'vegotcancerwhatthefuckican'tbelievemyluckbutalsowhen's
thisbellygonnashrinki'mprobablydreamingithinki'mgoingto
killmygrandmawiththisnews

I'm wheeled belly-first through A&E,
It's me, my mum, Jess and the porter
And over the beeping builds a crescendo of it's so fucking
loud
I think my mum's more overwhelmed than her daughter
As we move through the pain and the impatience of the
crowd
And as we get further it's like the patience gets shorter

peoplewithbandagesontheirheadsarestoodupsothatthepeople
withbandagesontheirlegscansitdowneverysinglepersonis
making at least some kind of noise it's sometimes talking
sometimes shouting crying wailing groaning beeping I think
some of these people might be beeping

I'm handed a form to fill in what's wrong with me
I tick the box that says cancer
Another ping on the bell of reality
We settle in the centre of A&E
Even the smell has a sound
They haven't found me a bed just yet
So I have to wait in between a man with a bloody nose
And my mum who's replying to messages she's starting to get
We've got to tell people, I suppose
And people are gonna go mental I bet.

It's past midnight all you can hear is talking why is no one
sleeping and that fucking beeping is keeping on and on and
on sometimes it gets louder and faster is that life support will
I ever be on life support my mum's speaking to Dad on the
phone he's crying

I've only ever seen Dad cry two times
Once was fine cos he was just having a tantrum about the
Glastonbury site crashing
The other time was at my grandpa's funeral
But to tell your dad not to worry about your cancer diagnosis
seems a crass thing
So I say come to London and soon we'll all
Be together. Okay, Dad? I'm doing okay. Just come first
thing.

I don't want to have this conversation again and again and
beep the phone is out of battery and is that beeping you or
my one Mum or is it the machines fucking hell I feel like it's
a soundtrack an underlay in the carpet of my brain right now
they've found you a bed now Rosa let's go up to the sixth
floor bloody hell people are beeping at me because I'm going
first, I feel bad for everyone because even a broken finger
fucking hurts beep I'm sorry beep but Dad will be here
tomorrow then we'll all beep together be together.

Together.

Beep.

Tomorrow.

Beep.

I've still got a hold on a tomorrow.

Beep.

I've still got an idea of together.
We go up in the lift and there's a shift
We leave the chaos and fluorescence in casualty
It's just my mum and I in the mirrors surrounding me
The pain is worse by the time we meet the nurse

Who whispers a list of medicines he will give me
Sits me on a bed
In a bay of a few women, all sleeping.
It's quieter in my head.
There is just this beeping.

ROSA *observes her surroundings in the semi-silent semi-dark. She sleeps.*

I am woken up suddenly by the sharp drawing-back of the blue curtains around my bed. It is still dark outside, and the lights haven't been turned on yet. About eight people walk in. This is my team. A doctor, a clinical nurse specialist, registrar, and more people whose job titles I don't understand introduce themselves.

DOCTOR NO BULLSHIT. Can you tell me on a scale of one to five how bad the pain is, Rosa?'

ROSA. I think for a minute. Kidney-stone pain was pretty bad. My tattoos were like a three. Being told I was wifey material but not worth committing to 'just at the moment' was definitely a five.

I'm gonna say a four.

DOCTOR NO BULLSHIT. We need to move you towards treatment as fast as possible so your situation doesn't get any worse, Rosa. We all wanted to come and discuss exactly what will be happening to you over the next few days. Are you ready?

My parents aren't here and I'm about as ready to receive medical information and terminology as I am to leap out of bed and start leading these doctors in an English country dance, but I nod.

*Words from the following monologue are blurry, the whole delivery is heightened and abstract.*

DOCTOR NO BULLSHIT. The liquid in your stomach is called ascites and it's caused by cancer on your lymph nodes means that liquid is not draining naturally which means we'll need to drain it here so we'll get the drain in, ascites out, all whilst keeping the pain in control, we'll get you on a combination of morphine, codrydamol, ibuprofen and regular paracetamol, then of course we'll need to take a biopsy to make sure that your tumour is not epithelial but a germ cell, as suspected, and whether it's a dysgerminoma or another strand, and of course we need to locate all the organs the cancer has spread to, those results will take a long time to come back, but as your tumour markers are extremely high we'll have to start chemotherapy straight away –

ROSA. Hang on, what? I was told last night I'd be having radiotherapy. Maybe surgery.

My hair.

DOCTOR NO BULLSHIT. No. If you have a germ-cell tumour, they take on a more liquid consistency – they won't respond to radiotherapy. The chemo, however has a good chance of working. So let's get you started with EP, which is made of eptoposide, and cisplatin. Then we'll look at adding bleomycin later on. We'll get you started on dexmethasone and ondansetron, steroids that will help with the sickness –

ROSA. I feel my long, red hair falling down my back like tears.

BRIDGET. Are you alright?

ROSA. It's the woman from the next bed. I look at her. She has no hair. I burst into tears.

She heaves herself up from her bed and sits with me on the edge of mine, and wraps me up in her arms.

I sob into her shoulder.

I'm sorry. I just found out I'm having chemotherapy and I didn't want to have it, it sounds so scary and I thought I was having radiotherapy and I only found out I had cancer on Thursday and my parents aren't here and I'm – I'm – I'm only twenty-three!

The woman is called Bridget, and she tells me about chemo and admits that, yes it's shit, and yes, you lose your hair, and yes, it damages your fertility. I suck up a huge, heaving breath that is threatening to be a scream.

BRIDGET. But it works, love. It's better than the other option.

ROSA. I let the tears out and I get snot all over her hospital gown.

I'm sorry.

She hugs me again.

BRIDGET. You have nothing to be sorry for.

ROSA. I've started to tell people about what's going on. Messages start to trickle in.

I get a message from Tinder Boy asking if I'm okay. I can't bring myself to reply. What an unfair position to put someone in. 'Hi, great first date, would you like the second one to be in hospital? I'm not allowed to eat or drink, but I'm sure they'd be able to sort you out with a juice box, and I'll give you a bit of my morphine if you're into that.'

I am so thirsty from the oral morphine. I have to be nil-by-mouth until they start to drain my stomach. I can't concentrate on anything else apart from the thick, dry tongue that is flopping around my mouth like a drunk slug in a fur coat.

Please can I drink something?

NURSE. No, Rosa. Just sip water and then spit it out. That will keep your mouth from getting dry. Nil-by-mouth means nil-by-mouth, I'm afraid.

*The drain is attached.*

Wow. That's filling up quickly. We'll have to keep checking your blood pressure to make sure you don't become ill.

More ill.

ROSA *has two cups. She sips and spits.*

*'Mumbo Jumbo' by Tierra Whack plays. She sips and spits.*

*She gets iller, and iller until:*

*The screens darken. She lies on the floor.*

ROSA. I've stopped feeling at this point. I don't feel anxiety. I don't feel fear. I don't ask questions. I let my mum hold my hand and do all the talking.

I haven't got enough of my own blood in my body to do anything but watch someone else's creep into my arm. I have a bruise the size of a melon on one hip from where the biopsy was taken, another on the opposite side from where the drain was attached. But my stomach looks even bigger than before it was drained. My legs are thick and bloated. My skin is milk, if milk was grey.

Alone, I remember how much I hated my body as a teenager.

I would watch myself grow and widen and fill with total disgust, mistaking puberty with becoming something unacceptable for a teenager to be: fat.

This is my body hating me back.

I promise. If we get better. I will never fuck you about again.

I will learn that what has just happened to me is the closest I have ever come to death.

I will learn that the attempt to drain the ascites from my stomach goes wrong, and accidentally drains so much blood that my haemoglobin drops to sixty-two. Which is nearly half of what it should be.

I will learn that the handful of painkillers, steroids, and anti-sickness medicine I'm taking three times a day can cause hallucinations and insomnia.

I will learn –

I.

I'm squinting through the half-light at my huge stomach, completely unshrunk by the drain, and see that between the two bruises on my hips, another bruise is forming below my belly button.

Shit.

I have a good imagination
Even without the added hallucinations
That I am unaware the medication
Has caused to flare
Inside my brain
So instead I have a fixation
On the stain
Below my belly button
And so I imagine
What this bruise could be.
Just a bruise?
Like the cancer was 'just bloating'
An irrational thought?
But the answer is floating through
And I don't think I just caught
My stomach on a door handle.

Thoughts are like flames,
And this bruise is a discarded cigarette on the forest ground
And my thoughts about the bruise
Have caught hold of dry leaves
And I remember
My mum is not with me.
The fire travels through until it catches on to the roots
Of where the leaves fall
The tree.
The tree –
The tree is the reason
The reason for it all
Why I'm here, why my mum has to be with me.
She has to be with me because
I've got cancer, oh my god I've got actual cancer.
And for the first time I have a chance to
properly process this
Because of drains
And blood
And passing out
And being sick

And telling people
And not telling people
And chemo plans
And holding hands
And crying
And trying to get on with it
Trying not to think about it
Trying not to die or
Trying not to catch fire
But once the flames are on the tree they keep spreading
And on to the next tree they're heading to the rest of the
forest
And trees are meant to produce oxygen
But I'm being set fire to again
Oxygen is not being produced
I can't breathe I can't breathe I actually cannot breathe and
it's more than just a bruise
I'm pressing my emergency button and a nurse is in my
room
She's holding my hand and telling me what to do

To get that breath back into my lungs.

It all hurts so much.

She squeezes my hand.

I'm just really scared.

She squeezes my hand.

It becomes a bit easier to take in some air.

Her name is Natalie.

She's not going anywhere.

Sleep is the final extinguishing of the fire.

I wake up.

I see my mum.

I smile.

I will learn that the reason I now have the energy to do this is because I have two brand-new units of A-positive blood pumping around my body.

I will learn that the blood belongs to someone healthy. Someone who exercises regularly.

Someone who is between seventeen and sixty-six years old, apparently. I bet they eat chia seeds. I bet they own a tennis skirt. Or could it be a man? Not that a man can't own a tennis skirt, but could it be a man's blood inside of me? Is that a thing? How long would it be before I start needing to wax my chest, or worse, using the phrase 'Not All Men'? Then again, Not All Men need to wax their chest.

But neither will I.

I will learn that chemo will make waxing of any body part completely unnecessary.

I will learn all of this soon.

But for now, I know my mum is here, and I feel like smiling. I feel... better.

Better in this sense means that I start to open my eyes for longer than five minutes at a time. Better in this sense means that I can turn my phone on. It means that the succession of bad days become peppered with good days. It means that I can start having visitors. My auntie, my mum, my dad crowd into my little quarantine, and before long my friends start to join. These are the good days. Rhi, Grace and Teb empty their bags onto my bed and out fall face masks, chocolate, three different kinds of lip balm and moisturisers. Fabien, Ed, Fred, Jack and Tomos lean up against the window and do impressions of each other, my nurses commenting on my good-looking friends every time they come to administer more pain relief. On the good days, the room is full of people, my people, and everyone's laughing and talking to each other, and we're not talking about my illness even though it's all around us. My lack of energy doesn't matter, I can just lie back and smile as their voices ping over me. The bad days happen when I'm alone. When my pain scale is past a five, when I'm tired, and I'm fed up.

My dad comes to visit me on one of these bad days where all I can do is stare at the TV, unable to concentrate on anything other than *Gordon Ramsay's Kitchen Nightmares*.

My dad asks me why I don't listen to music.

We've always shared this really religious love of music. He bought me my first CD – which was Busted's first album – on the condition that he could buy me Billie Holiday and a compilation of Motown's greatest hits. That's also kind of been the attitude to my life he's adopted. Whenever I make a questionable life choice, he lets me do what I want but is there to offer a couple of really good alternatives to turn to when I realise my bad judgement later in life.

That's what he's doing now. Less bad TV, healing music instead.

I can't.

I haven't listened to music since getting to hospital.

It's probably the longest I've not listened to music, ever. It was always playing in my house growing up, and then always in my headphones when I got my first Walkman, MiniDisc, iPod. I discovered jazz with my dad, dance music with my friends, hip hop with my ex-boyfriend, Christmas songs and hymns with my grandma, the magic of the musicals with my other grandma, folk music with my granddad.

But here the music has stopped. Because it won't be healing.

The idea of listening to a song physically hurts me, almost as much as the ascites. It feels like mourning. Like pining for something that I can't have, even though I can – I could press play any time. But I'll be reminded of where I was before this. I'll be reminded of my family. Or of a gig where I danced with complete abandon. Or a DJ night where someone told me I had the most beautiful hair they'd ever seen. Or all the love songs I would never get to relate to, because I'd not got a chance to be in love. There's this song, it's called 'Tadow'. By an artist called Masego. And it's called 'Tadow' because that's the sound when you see someone who you fall in love with straight away, you know? Like TADOW. You see them and it hits you like TADOW. And I used to listen to it thinking. Oh. I can't wait for my TADOW. It'll happen. And now. For the first time I've been hit with a what if it won't? What if I never fall in love?

ROSA *dances to no music. During this, she runs her hands through her hair. It starts to come out.*

I want to tell you about this girl I meet the day I shave my head.

Upon arrival at the hospital for my second chemo, my hair is falling out onto my jumper and more is being pulled away every time I take my scarf off.

Every time I pull a brush through it, the loose hair tangles into the rest of it, and there's a constant matted clump at my neck.

As I sit waiting for the doctor, I am surrounded by the threads of my illness. I wrap one around my forefinger and watch the tip of it turn red. I feel my pulse strain against the strand of hair.

There is a girl sat up in the bed opposite, on top of the covers like me, and I smile at her over my strangled finger.

As is the custom with hospitals she seems to be waiting,
She's not joining in with the guy she's with's agitated pacing,
But sitting.
A patient patient.
And she smiles at me a smile that's so much more than just teeth-gritting,
Life bursts out of her mouth towards me.
And I smile back, feeling honoured she hasn't ignored me.

When the guy she's with leaves, he grins too,
Nods to me and says 'my girlfriend wants to speak to you.'
I hear her voice
'Don't be a dick!'

But she makes the choice
And hobbles across to my bed, covered in the red
Strands of my hair
Hey
I'm Rai
You okay?
It's nice to see someone my age here
Fuck, I didn't mean to say
Nice
It's just everyone else is
Twice
As old, it's hard to relate
I get it I say and we begin to relate
Our cancers are different but the story's the same
Both girls trying to work in the artists' game,
Rai is a writer,
And her shoulder got tighter
Till they found the little blighter in her shoulder
A sarcoma
In her bone and soft tissue
Her issue is it's spread
To her lungs and her brain,
But the chemo will shrink it, our story's the same.
I tell her I'm worried about my hair falling out
She puts her hand on mine
We've got bigger things to worry about,
And anyway, you're fine, I know you're gonna rock it,
So before my chemo starts,
I think, okay. It's probably time to chop it.

I am granted two hours' leave before I'm plugged in, to head
to a King's Cross hairdresser. I tell the man at the desk I've
got an odd request. He looks up. He's bald. I pull my beanie
off and show him that it's full of my hair.

I'm, uh, well, I'm having chemotherapy at the moment and
it makes your hair just fall out loads and I just think
I should, um. I want to shave it all. It's just annoying me.
I just want it off.

The hairdresser takes a second. Then he smiles, shows me to a chair and he puts a gown on me. I've been in a hairdresser's chair and gown hundreds of times, grinning at them in the mirror and telling them to take a bit, cut a fringe, put some blonde in, make me feel sexy, make me feel new. This time, I look at the electric razor and wait for the hairdresser to plug it in.

When it's over, I look at myself. I thought I'd cry, or laugh. I don't feel anything.

The hairdresser brushes the remains from my neck and takes me up to the desk. I hold out my card. He holds my hand instead. 'It's free for you today. Whenever you want. It's always free for you.'

A woman walks past us, I assume she is the manager. She does a double-take. 'That's a big change, sweetheart!'

I think of Rai.

'I've had bigger.'

Back to the hospital, to show Rai and thank her for the bravery
I knew I had it in me but it was something that she gave me
But I return to the bay and her bed is empty,
She's been moved
To a private room
To keep on top of her pain
When I was at my worst, they did the same
I'll wait till next chemo to see her again.

*Resolution Number Two comes up onto the screen.*

My scans are now showing my tumour is shrinking. The chemo is working. It's destroying the cancer. But it's also destroying me. My immune system is completely compromised, so on the occasions I can go home, I can't leave the house. But even if I could, I wouldn't have the energy. The steroids used to combat this fatigue cause huge water retention in my face and the bald, red girl I see in the mirror is not one I recognise. I feel horrific; I look horrific; I feel horrific. Every time I start to climb back from the incredible dips that chemo causes, I have to go in for another round. A week of lying horizontally, hooked up to a drip full of poison. Another week of bad days.

And I don't want to talk about that.

But I have to remember the people who pull the bad days out of me, and hug and kiss and make them laugh until they are good days. My family. The nurses. My friends. You don't know them, but I want you to. From the minute I got diagnosed, my friends have been there. I have to remember the time that everyone visited me on Valentine's Day, and brought me heart-shaped balloons. The thirty-minute epic video that Rhi made for me, full of messages from our friends. The time after the failed drain attempt, after the blood transfusions, after I'd just started my first chemo where –

*She thinks.*

Grace falls into my hospital room, and into my arms for a hug. She's rushing in before she has to go and warm up for the matinee of the play she's in. She comes to see me nearly every day before her show. She's followed closely by Fabien, who explodes into the room wearing sunglasses and clutching a box of paracetamol, hungover from the night before. He's characteristically still full of zeal though, and knocks over my side table whilst showing us the dance he was teaching everyone at the club last night.

Grace needs to go, but she's waiting to see Teb. They literally saw each other yesterday when they both came to visit, which seems weird, but I suppose there's something about my illness that has brought us even closer together. When Teb finally turns up, the room feels full – we're all talking over each other and laughing, and although I'm tired, these visits keep me going.

'I need to go,' says Grace.

I open my arms to give her a hug, but Fab intercepts it, and comes towards me brandishing his phone, telling me about some video he's seen that I need to watch.

Fabien's boundless energy can sometimes translate to not knowing how to read a room.

Er. Yeah. Fab, I'm just saying goodbye to Grace.

But Grace cuts in – 'Yeah, Rosa, watch it before I leave. I don't mind.'

I lie back on my pillows and concede. If Grace thought it was rude, she would have said so.

Okay.

*A video message from* LOUIS THEROUX *plays on the screen.*

LOUIS THEROUX. Hi, this is Louis Theroux. Coming to you from sunny Los Angeles, with a message for Rosa. Rosa, through my back channels – that's an odd phrase, isn't it? – through secret sources, it's come to my attention that you've had some bad news, and I just wanted to let you know that I will be thinking of you, and wishing you all the best at this difficult time. Stay strong, and just know that there are lots of people who love you, and are rooting for you. Best of luck.

*The video finishes.*

ROSA. That afternoon, I walk down to the hospital café, and eat cake. I don't need a nap afterwards.

Louis Theroux and love. Better than any steroid out there.

DOCTOR NO BULLSHIT. The scan results all came back clear, Rosa. Your blood tests are looking brilliant. You're all clear. No evidence of disease.

ROSA *makes a noise that sounds like happiness and joy at receiving the news. She is almost crying. But she is not.*

ROSA. And the celebrations start. I drink champagne at three in
the afternoon because I'm better! I order a takeaway that
night because I'm well! I have a party with my friends to
celebrate me being all better. I dance, like I always said
I would once I was well! I am ready to grab life by the balls!
I'm alive! Nothing will ever bother me again. Nothing can
ever compare to what I've been through! This experience has
made me brave! I am well! I am alive! I am better.

I am well.
I am better.
All is better.
All is well.

*As if from before.*

I'm really struggling to know what story I want to tell, but
I know I need to tell it.

It's so important to tell your story.

Because otherwise people will keep asking you, 'So what
you doing next? You survived, didn't you? I bet nothing ever
bothers you now you've been through that!'

And if you say you survived, and don't thrive, people might
write you off, and then stop caring. So I need to get cracking.
For other people. Because I've always been good at this,
being okay.

Being strong. Getting on with it. So people are expecting it
of me. So I should get on with it.

I should sit here now and tell you about the list of medicines
I was sent home with. All their names, long and complicated,
so you would marvel at the detail and the wonders of modern
medicine. I should talk you through the science. The
intricacies of my operation to remove my fallopian tube, my
ovary and that fucking omentum. I should talk about my
odds. My prognosis. You'd be like, 'Oooh.' But also, 'Ohhh.'

I'm also tempted to tell you that Tinder Boy came to visit
me. And stayed by my side. And we got to know each other
through every blood transfusion, he stroked my hair as it

fell out, and he listened to me, without trying to give
advice, he just listened, and was there. But of course he
wasn't – I WhatsApped him about a month in to update
him, and he left my message on read.

Which is fine. But it's not the perfect rounding-out to this
story that I'm wishing I could tell you. It's not a satisfying
tying-up of loose ends.

It's not telling you, step by step all the way from the Louis
Theroux video all the way up to the date I got the all-clear.
And telling you about that day, and how it was the best day
of my life. It's not telling you that because it wasn't.

The day I got medically issued with no evidence of disease,
the all-clear, put into remission, was not the day it was all
over and done with. It wasn't 'back to normal'.

It was the start of building a 'new normal' from nothing, but
having to hold on to the fact that I'm not allowed to have my
old normal back.

And the new normal is lots of things. It's sometimes being
hit in the face with paralysing fear.

Overwhelming sadness. Burning rage. And being told, that's
PTSD. And you're like, oh shit, I am one of those people
with PTSD. It's suddenly thinking about your fertility, all the
time. Which seems so unfair, to have to think about that at
twenty-three, when I can't even get to the second date
without getting cancer. It's wondering, what if my cancer
comes back? What then? Is this mole cancer? Is this lump
cancer? Is this bruise cancer? Am I going to die normally or
of cancer? It's meeting people like Bridget, who show you
such intense kindness and disappear, and you don't know
where they are now. I never got to thank her. These people
just appear and diasppear as quickly as they are admitted and
discharged. And. The new normal is. It's meeting other
young people with cancer and – And them – And how they
don't – they can't always – you've got this new group of
friends but the difference is is when you meet them you have
to say to yourself –

She puts her hand on mine.
We've got bigger things to worry about.
I come back to show her and thank her for the bravery
I knew I had it in me but it was something that she gave me
But I return to the bay and her bed is empty,
She's been moved
To a private room
To keep on top of her pain
When I was at my worst, they did the same
So I wait till next chemo to see her again.

I come back and ask a nurse do you know if Rai's here?
I met her last month and I wanted to see her.
Tell her they've done scans and the tumour is shrinking
And when we're both done with treatment I'm thinking
We should write about it.
About the fight of it.
It'd be – nice, wouldn't it?

And the nurse says,
'Oh, Rosa.
Rai died.'

And it's like the light and life that shined
Out of her mouth on that first day is suddenly in my eye.

Don't cry.
She had so much love by her side
That day.

I didn't even really know her enough to say
She was my friend
I know it must sound insane
But I thought that our stories were going to be the same.
I would get better
And so would she
And then she'd write fourteen best-sellers
And I'd be the new flea
bag.
I'm sad.
Because why was it me?

Who got to survive?
I can't think about that stuff cos it'll eat me up inside
But I had to tell you about Rai.
Not my hair, or my medication regimes, or the day-to-day.
This is what cancer did mainly.
Even after no disease is remaining,
This is what stays
The people like Rai.
The ones you meet and as you do you have to say
To yourself
We might not be long for this earth,
Is it worth
Making these little, live connections?
When there's no guarantee that we'll survive all the same
sections?
Is it worth making a friend with cancer?
I end Rai's story with a resounding answer.
Yes.
Because I want to thank them for the bravery
I knew I had it in me but it's something that they gave me.

And if my cancer comes back, I have to remember.

When I do die – which I will – I have to remember.

I have to remember what I remember.

All the memories. Everything I remember is what I am, and
I have to remember it's been fucking brilliant.

I remember so much fucking brilliance. Even the bad was
brilliance.

I remember plastic toy animals going missing in the grass.
I remember clambering onto a step by the sink to spit my
toothpaste into the basin, and there went a tooth. I remember
putting my ear against my little brother's tummy to see what
it sounded like inside. I remember crying my eyes out when
my mum told me that it wasn't the real Harry Potter writing
me letters, it was her all along. I remember the first gold star
that shone next to my work. The red pen of a teacher who
I thought must know everything about the world but

probably felt more lost than her Year 5 class did. I remember pushing the table back and dancing in my living room to Justin Timberlake but I only had one dance move and it was this. I remember stretching my eyelid taut so I could scrape the first trace of eyeliner on my waterline. I remember the smell of ammonia as I tried blonde. The first taste of alcohol and then the second immediately afterwards. I remember kissing a boy for the first time, his lips tense and discovered against mine. I remember kissing a boy for the second time, it was a lot more wet.

I remember thinking my heart was broken and watching every episode of *CSI* ever made was the only thing that could fix it. I remember forgetting I was enough.

I remember my dad taking me for drives and to art galleries and telling me 'I get sad too and it's okay.'

I remember the first time I cried to music.

I remember the first time I kissed to music.

I remember the first time I had sex to music.

I remember the first time I made love to music.

I remember the first time I downloaded music onto a computer and I'm so sorry but it was 'Now You're Gone' by Basshunter.

I remember meeting all of my best friends, one by one by one by one. I remember bringing each of them to meet my family and knowing that really there was no difference between them at all.

I remember feeling.

I remember holding feelings in my hands and my heart and my eyes and my soul. I have denied my soul my entire life. Because I didn't think it meant anything. But my soul means all of what I just said. All of my memories. I've glided through the world like a cloth and picked up the fluff and dust that might not always seem the most poignant, the most life-changing. But it's part of me forever. No matter what happens. There's no tumour on my soul.

I am not better.

But *things* are better.

So maybe I am, a bit.

I have been in love. This whole time. And, no, there is no difference between love and in love. Because I have been deep, deep, deep, within, inside, surrounded by, submerged in, in, in, in love. So plunged into it that I thought I'd never had it. So deep under the surface that I couldn't hear that that was all I needed. It's all I need. When – if – how I die. I will have known what it feels like to be in love. Fucking brilliant.

*'Everything Is Borrowed' by The Streets starts to play.*

*On the screen, the resolutions appear, one by one.*

*I WILL GET MY PRIORITIES RIGHT.*

*Afterwards, a montage of all the videos that were sent by friends, family, Louis Theroux.*

*I WILL TAKE BETTER CARE OF MY BODY.*

ROSA *gives herself a huge, knackered hug, and takes a sip of water.*

*I WILL MAKE SOME REALLY GOOD ART.*

*The End.*

# TAKE CARE

*A Verbatim Play*

Zoë Templeman-Young & Sam McLaughlin

*To all the unheard carers*
*To Mumma and Mumkins*

## CATHY LYNCH

Driven by the fight for social change, Cathy Lynch was one of the three original devisers of *Take Care*. She is also a podcast producer and writer.

## SAM McLAUGHLIN

Sam McLaughlin is an actor, theatre-maker and improviser based in Bristol. Since graduating from Royal Conservatoire of Scotland, Sam has performed with Missing Pieces and is a company member of the Bristol Improv Theatre's flagship shows: *This Is Your Musical* and *The Bish Bosh Bash*.

## ZOË TEMPLEMAN-YOUNG

Zoë Templeman-Young is an actor, director and theatre-maker. She trained at the Royal Academy of Dramatic Art. Her professional credits as an actress include *Mary Stuart* (Almeida).

*Take Care* was first performed at VAULT Festival, London, on 10 March 2020.

| | |
|---|---|
| *Director* | Zoë Templeman-Young |
| *Dramaturgs* | Sam McLaughlin, |
| | Zoë Templeman-Young |
| *Sound Design* | Matt Kirk |
| *Lighting Design* | Catja Hamilton |

*At the time of going to print the play was still to be cast.*

A previous, shorter version of the play was performed at the Gielgud Studio, RADA Festival 2019, with the following cast:

Cynthia Emeagi
Hal Geller
Danny Hughes
Charlotte Keith
Zoë Templeman-Young

Thank you to all of the individuals who trusted us with their stories, without which this play could not exist. These consist of: informal carers, private/agency carers, care managers, NHS doctors and nurses, NHS officials, psychologists, activities coordinators, activists, security guards, family and friends.

Special thanks to: ARJO, Arts Council England, Caroline Allouf, Carers Network, Carers Support Centre, Carers Trust, Felicity Green, Granny Val, Hannah Tookey, Katharine Farmer, Kentish Town Community Centre, Kerry Irvine, LondonADASS Improvement Programme, Nick Hern Books, Pound Arts (special shout-out to Martin), Sarah Stacey, Upstart Theatre, VAULT Festival, Warwick University.

*S.M, Z T-Y.*

**Characters**
*in order of appearance*

PAM, *accent: South-west London*
RUTH, *accent: Essex*
CHARLIE, *accent: Estuary/West London*
SHARON, *accent: MLE*
KEIR, *accent: Kent*
SAM, *accent: Kent*
GINA, *accent: Estuary*
GRAHAM, *accent: heightened RP/Lewes*
SOFIE, *accent: Bristol*
LYDIA, *accent: Russian*
ROBERT, *accent: Cockney*
SARAH, *accent: RP/Bristol*
PAULINE, *accent: Cockney*
ROBIN, *accent: RP*
KATHY, *accent: RP*
EMMA, *accent: Estuary*
STEPH, *accent: Cork*

**Note on Text**

All the text spoken by named characters is verbatim.

Some names of interviewees have been changed for legal reasons.

All politicians/political commentators are voice-overs.

All voice-overs feature the person's actual voice.

All text is direct address to the audience.

/ denotes an interruption by the following character.

This production is performed by a maximum of five actors.

This selection of interviews were specifically chosen to feature in the VAULT Festival 2020 production.

*Two* PERFORMERS *stand onstage.*

*They talk directly to the audience.*

NARRATOR. The stories you are about to hear are true stories. This isn't one of those times a precursor will flash up saying:

NARRATOR 2. Based on a true story.

NARRATOR. Which actually normally means ninety per cent was fictional.

NARRATOR 2. Nothing wrong with that.

NARRATOR. No. But it can be misleading. We want to say, upfront, that our stories are one-hundred-per-cent true. From real people, from all around the country.

NARRATOR 2. And even us.

NARRATOR. Oh yeah, us. We're doing this because we used to be carers.

NARRATOR 2. We have both worked either professionally or personally as carers of the elderly. And our two voices join the thousands of others from around this country. The voices of people who have reached out to us and felt compelled to tell their stories.

NARRATOR. Because they, like us, feel frustrated, angry, confused – about the state of the care system for older people. And how carers are treated.

And we know that when you look after an older person –

NARRATOR 2. It is bloody hard.

NARRATOR. It is exhausting.

NARRATOR 2. But it's also hilarious and ridiculous. And sometimes makes you laugh so much a little bit of wee comes out.

NARRATOR. And it's fine if that happens because the person you're looking after normally wees themselves all the time.

NARRATOR 2. So you're in the same boat.

NARRATOR. You're equals.

*Beat.*

NARRATOR 2. We're all planning on growing old right? Which means we all expect to be looked after. So it's time to sit up and listen to these carers. Time to support the supporters.

NARRATOR. So let's start.

NARRATOR 2. You probably recognise this voice –

DAVID CAMERON. We made a promise to people, that if elected, we would not cut the NHS, we'd put extra money into the NHS and that is what we've done.

NARRATOR. Now you're going to hear some new voices. And they're just as real as that one, and just as important.

*Fade to…*

*A living room.*

*It is decorated in bright Christmas decorations.*

*There is a miniature Christmas tree yet to be decorated.*

PAM *wears a reindeer hat.*

PAM. On Christmas Day, I went to my mum's to pick her up to take her to a restaurant – we was gonna eat out. And when she opened the door to me I could see why she hadn't been letting me in and I could see that she obviously had a huge problem, cos she was hoarding so much you couldn't move in there. And I just knew that, you know, this is a serious problem. And I knew that, you know, this, her mind had gone.

*Fade to…*

*A homely home.*

*Washing hangs on a wash rail.*

*There is an incredible spread on the table – biscuits, sandwiches, cakes.*

RUTH *sits, her make-up and mirror in front of her.*

RUTH. I started caring for my mother in two thousand and... two. She went in for a hip operation, when she came out it became very apparent that she was never, ever going to be able to look after herself, on her own, again. And that's when it all started. It just started from there.

*Fade to...*

*A hospital waiting area.*

CHARLIE *sits, dressed all in black. She has a Spotlight bag next to her.*

*She holds a coffee in one hand, glasses in the other.*

CHARLIE. People can sort of get that idea that, 'Oh you're really nice, and this is what you do and...' It just kinda pisses me off, cos I just think, 'I do this cos I love my mum and that's it.' It's no – I'm not naturally, you know, it wasn't something that I naturally was, wanted to do all my life or whatever, like, do you know what I mean?

*Newsflash.*

NARRATOR. Back in 1997 Tony Blair said:

TONY BLAIR. I would say to the country, that previous Labour Governments have done well by Britain's pensioners – always – and we will do well by them again.

NARRATOR. Jump forward and between 2005 and 2010 public funding for older people's social care stagnated. In March 2010 Andy Burnham, Labour's Health Secretary, says:

ANDY BURNHAM. If you cut social care – in the end, the collapse of social care will drag down the NHS.

NARRATOR. The Labour Government proposes a National Care Service, which would provide services free at the point of need. Decisions on how this would be funded are not clarified. And the policy is dropped following the election of the Coalition Government.

PAM *enters, holding a banner of David Cameron's pledge:*

'I'll cut the deficit, not the NHS.'

*She turns it over to reveal a protest banner:*

'Fuck the Tories.'

PAM. I adored it during the elections, mixing with all those Left wingers, I just thought, I'm at home here! That's right! Exactly. Cos like I never, I always shied away from cameras, I didn't like my photos taken cos I'm highly critical, if I see a photo of myself now – hate it! So in my, dancing and what have you, I always shy away, shy away from any camera and I hate it if one pops up somewhere like 'Ooooh'. But for the first time in my life when I was out with the Labour people erm, during the campaign I thought I was proud to be with my people, in front of the camera – do you want to see, I might have a picture? I was a bit fat then, cos I joined Weight Watchers, so I still feel a bit bad.

*Fade to…*

*An open-plan sitting room, TV on in the background.*

*There are notes all around the room, stuck on cupboards and doors.*

SHARON *is in a T-shirt and shorts. She has an 'I LOVE MUM' tattoo on her arm.*

SHARON. Yeah, I've got a brother, he does his own thing. And I've got a sister that's very helpful. (*Laughs.*)

But I just said to myself… without thinking! When she was in hospital, 'Oh what's gonna happen to – Oh I'll just care for her.' And they said 'But you'll have to give up work,' I goes, 'Yeah.'

I worked for London Underground. Yeah, I did, I did. I started off as a station assistant, and now I thought, there's so many avenues that you can go, I thought no I'm not gonna be a train operator – ticket office is much warmer. (*Laughs*.) Yeah, I loved it actually.

But I left when Social Services was preparing us to come home. So that's, you know, after about two years, they got rid of the ticket offices right? So yeah. Getting her home was a nightmare, oh my God – (*Head in hands*.) nightmare. Social Services dragged their feet, they really annoyed me big time because you know what? I, um, left my job in 2009, February two-thousand – hoping that my mum would be home by September, she wasn't. Yeah? I didn't have my mum home, back, till... September... 2010. So it took a year. I was a year out of work. So can you imagine all the problems they caused me? All the preparation Social Service's side. The hospital was fine. It was Social Services. I can't stand them. I don't like them. Sorry, I'm saying it like it – I hate them! With a passion. Hate is a very strong word. I shouldn't say them... It's the system. Okay, let me correct myself. It's the system. Yeah?

*Fade out.*

NARRATOR. There are seven million carers in the UK today and this number is rising. Seven million works out at one in three. Chances are that even if you are not a carer yourself, you know someone who is.

*Fade back to...*

*A hospital waiting room.*

CHARLIE. I was sitting there with my mum when she was in hospital once and – this was the third night I was sleeping in the hospital. And I went into the room and they have these, there was this, this TV's on the really high up – Mum was in a room on her own and they were so sweet to me, bringing me tea and biscuits. And this one nurse was so lovely she was like 'Oh my God,' you know, 'You're never getting any rest!' – She sort of put these pillows up for me and she – tea and biscuits.

So I thought I'll try and put something on, you know, like *Big Bang* or my mum quite likes, uhm, the, *IT Crowd*, the Richard – the... So I thought even if she can't hear it, she can hear the laughter. So I'm up there tryna change the channels – and I dunno how, but I got a porn channel and I thought, 'Why is that on in the hospital?!' It's bizarre, it was just the bizarrest night of my life – and my mum's a very prayerful Irish Catholic, you know, that is not something she'd enjoy, you know. And I was like, tryna switch it off and I put the volume up! And a nurse came in and she sort of went, 'Uhmm,' she was very practical, she went, 'Is this, was a, what were you trying to get?' And I was just like, 'Not this, not this, not this!' But whatever I did looked wrong, I was standing on a chair so it looked like – (*Laughs.*) yeah exactly! And tea and biscuits, cushions around and I was just like – and they were making all these sounds – yeah!

*Fade to...*

*A sitting room.*

KEIR *is sitting on the couch eating crackers and cheese.*

SAM *is sitting on a pillow on the floor, back against the radiator.*

SAM *is wearing a nurse's tunic.* KEIR *is in work-out gear.*

KEIR. I've got my mouth full. Hmm! We are called in... (*Laughs.*) on a personal safety consultancy basis to deliver training. (*Laughs.*) My job title's just a Security Trainer. Or Personal Safety Trainer. Yeah, yeaah... So what it actually is is Control and Restraint. But, because it's 2019 now, we call it Positive Holding (*Smiling.*) or Safe Holding. Yeah. Or Clinical Holding. Because it sounds more... more fluffy.

Oh, that often patients will lash out at certain staff and it might be because they've not, not really been explained what's about to happen. Erm. So one example's where staff had been called up to help subdue a patient because he was, er, lashing out and whilst they were talking to him – and he, he'd calmed down completely and he'd got dementia, but whilst he calmed down, the nurse just came up to the side of him and erm, tried to take his temperature by putting the thing in his ear (*Smiling*.) without communicating with him at all – just put it straight in. And he immediately lashed out again. Because he didn't expect it.

SAM. Pretty sure anyone would do that.

KEIR. Yeah... Know what I mean? Even, even if you were talking to someone and they walked round and they put something in your ear. (*Laughing*.) Wet willy. Wet willy! / Lucky you!

SAM (*laughing*). Wet willy!

KEIR. Yeah he was smashing the room up and um, they weren't trained or allowed to restrain him, so to stop him from attacking any other patients or themselves, they just held the door shut and like barricaded the door until he calmed down. Mmm. It's weighing up outcome. If you let him out, what might happen? What's the worst-case scenario? If you don't let him out, what's the worst-case scenario? And why. With me they learn to balance the outcomes and the impacts of their decisions.

With all elderly patients, individuals, you have to... be very gentle. Like, hold, rather than, and yeah, the force has to be proportionate to the... individual. You can't even hold them in a way that, if they... resist, will cause them pain. It's literally very gentle. Like, yeah.

SAM (*holding up her hands*). Squirrel paws!

KEIR. Say it again?

SAM. Squirrel paws!

KEIR. Squirrel paws. Is that what you were taught?

SAM. Squirrel paws! If you ever touch a patient, your thumb has to be close to your hand because that's the bit that does the grabby bit. And it stops you from grabbing. So you only support someone through that action.

KEIR. Oooh!

SAM. Squirrel paws!

*Both laugh.*

*Fade to…*

*Outside a house.*

*It's after a shift.* GINA *is wearing a pink care uniform and Crocs.*

*She is having a cigarette.*

GINA (*breath*). Orh, I started as a carer when I was – er – fourteen-and-a-half. Yes. Mm. (*Tuts.*) Errr because – (*Tuts.*) erm my father had – died and that and errr my mum couldn't afford pocket money and in those days you did work in shops and things from fourteen? A girl came up to me, into the playground, and said, erm, 'I heard you're' – Tina her name was, I remember it, I was sitting on the grass with my friends, and er she said 'I hear you're looking for a job', and, that was it.

No, I've had my moments, yeah, but it's, yeah. I was, ohhhh, I was about twenty-six, before I moved up here, I was twenty-six, I was in a rest home, I was really, aaaaahh, I always got taught, if you get annoyed, because not all clients are nice, is to leave the room. And I, and I left the room, and I – and I stuck my tongue out. I felt soo, I felt sooo, I felt so, awful, yeah, it's upset me now, because what a thing for her to huh, sorry, she had to see me go 'Eurrgh' and walkin' away, do you know what I mean? I should have just left the room, just left the room, but I had to have the last – (*Sniffs.*) and that, that taught me. If you're not helping them, you just walk away.

If people have their advocates, they have a voice if they haven't-got-a-voice-themselves. The people that haven't got family, or loved ones, or someone to look out for them, they are the vulnerable and they are the ones, they are the ones open for abuse.

*Fade out.*

NARRATOR. It's a job that most people think is pretty
thankless. So let's do some maths, let's get money involved,
and ask – how much do carers get paid in this country?

*Fade back to…*

*A homely home.*

RUTH. Wuw, the money I receive from the state, is a very
generous fifty-five pounds a week. Which considering that's
seven days a week, twenty-four-seven, works out at very,
very good value. If I put my mother into a home, it would be
a minimum of seven hundred and forty pounds, a week.
Seven hundred and forty pounds, over a hundred pounds a
day, which I'm doing for less than a fiver.

*Fade to…*

*A garden in the summer.*

GRAHAM *is sat at the table, drinking green tea.*

*He is incredibly well-dressed.*

GRAHAM. So here's an issue, controversial here. So agencies
charge fifteen pounds or twenty pounds an hour and the carer
gets paid seven pounds ninety-two. Now work that one out,
with the amount of people getting cared for in this country, at
home. The care agencies are making a lot of money, what's
happened to that money? I don't know, it's not been invested
in education so, so there's an issue there and there's an issue
there…

*Fade back to…*

*A sitting room.*

SAM *is sitting on a pillow on the floor, back against the
radiator.*

SAM. Yeah, so… There… is a company called Bank that are
employed by the NHS as a separate company and then… we
have messages go out, through Bank, asking us to work in
our place of work – in the same hospital, same ward, same

uniform (*Smiling*.) same people I work with (*Breath*.) but it gets taxed as a second job.

*Beat.*

I can do a… twelve-hour shift, eight hours of it being normal hours, and then four hours of it being overtime or Bank. But then I'll get taxed on the Bank, which will then take away all that money for the four hours, so I've worked four hours for free basically.

No idea, I think it's… just to do with… money. For the NHS. But, the people who actually do the work don't see any of the money. Yeah. For any staff across the NHS.

*Fade out.*

NARRATOR. It was estimated that in 2018 there were six-point-five million 'informal' carers in the UK.

NARRATOR 2. Informal carers are family or loved ones who may have no professional training for the work they do. This number is growing, mostly due to the rising cost of care homes.

NARRATOR. But for some, it is an outright choice to keep their loved ones in their homes – to look after them in a familiar space. And that's what happened with my family.

NARRATOR 2. And mine.

NARRATOR. And I wouldn't have changed it for the world.

NARRATOR 2. Me neither.

NARRATOR. And do you know why?

NARRATOR 2. Because older people can be fucking hilarious.

*Fade back to…*

*An open-plan sitting room, TV is still on in the background.*

SHARON. Oh my god, here we go. Yesterday, we was in Waitrose – my mum doesn't understand. We saw a – a dwarf, a short person. She go 'LOOO, LOO-LOO-LOO-LOO-

LOOOO!' I thought, 'MUM!' I goes, 'Yeah, but it's a person.' She go 'BUT LOOLOOOO –' (*Quietly.*) she doesn't understand.

Jeez.

But my mum has respect for, anybody, anybody in uniform. With the priest she's like 'Hello, Father, how are you?' – Totally different! 'Yes, Father, yes' –

*Fade back to…*

*A homely home.*

RUTH *is sat at the table.* SOFIE, *her daughter, is putting sandwiches out on a plate.*

*She hands them round the audience.*

RUTH. She gradually got worse and worse when she put all her clothes on inside out. And when that – I say inside out, I mean the skirt on first, the blouse on first, the bra over the top, the slip over the top and the knickers over everything, you see. So we, we, we got to the stage where at first, you thought 'How am I gunna cope with this? And I c– I'll march her back in and I'll make her put her clothes on in the right order.' And I thought, 'Well why?' She's in here, nobody's gonna know, and she's happy. So we let her do whatever she wanted. So she wore a bright-orange fluorescent coat once that she stole off my son, from the Royal Mail, and she went round in that cos orange and green were her favourite colours, and she was fluorescent in this beautiful jacket – she wouldn't let that go.

But we had a few problems, because my mother was a rebel when she was young and she didn't like being told what to do. And her favourite trick was waiting for the postman, and then posting the letters back out! That was such fun! And he would put them through, and she would put them back out, and we had to put an outside postbox up, we had to Sellotape the letterbox up and write 'PLEASE PUT EVERYTHING OVER THERE' and all this. So, we just changed things when they became apparent.

The Alzheimer's turns things on and off so she kept, walking
along and then bobbing. We couldn't understand what was
going on. It was the Alzheimer's trying to stop her walking –
she kept bobbing. So, for a few months I ha– had, when I
said to her 'Swas time for beds.' I had to go behind her and
put my arms round her and we walked together, like this
four-legged weird person, with two heads to bed, so that she
didn't bob and fall over, see, so we would walk –

SOFIE. Oh god, she fell, she, I tried to get her up once and she
– just – wuh – she cuz she / she –

RUTH. She was on the floor.

SOFIE. She very much liked just being where she was – so if
she was in bed, she liked being in bed and didn't necessarily
wanna get up. But if she was in the chair, she was in the
chair, she wouldn't wanna get up –

RUTH. And she slid, didn't she?

SOFIE. So when it came to transitions, that was always an
argument – yeah – so I was like 'No, c'mon, we need to get
to bed.' So we've done the row, we've done the like – 'No
you have to, please, it's time for bed Nan!' And she was just
be like, 'No, I'm not going!' And, er, so we eventually like,
I'd managed to like, convince her that 'Perhaps it's a good
idea?' And, I'd like got her up and she was like – but
halfway – and her balance wasn't in the exactly the right
place and so she slowly like sunk to the floor. And she was
big –

RUTH. She was a big girl.

SOFIE. And I was like, I was just like 'Hoo-ohh' – just try'na
like, dance her like slowly to the floor but also just being like
'NO, S'NAN, GET UP, UP, UP!' And so then she was just
on the floor –

RUTH. Laid out, like a slab.

SOFIE. And then she was like sat on my, like feet – up like that
– so like, to, for her back and I was like 'Nan, we need to get

you up.' And she was like 'La, la, la,' like lovin' life on the
floor and, er (*Laughs.*) and so I just like, laid her down
gently so she was just laid on the floor and... I was like,
wary of not tryna like, wrench her back or wrench mine. But
the floor is really slippy, so I ended up just like walking my
nan round the floor... and it's because she'd forgotten how to
walk a minute and that's what it was...

RUTH. People must have thought we were nuts if they'd even
seen through the windows – sliding this old lady up and
down the, uh, up and down the floor – zzzd, zzzd!

SOFIE. Yeah, in a high-vis jacket, yeah!

*Fade to...*

*A living room.*

ROBERT *is sat in an oversized armchair.*

*Books are piled everywhere. A piano is in the corner. A cat is
asleep on a rug.*

*There is a picture of the Queen smiling coyly directly to
camera, on the wall behind* ROBERT.

LYDIA. Robert has memory problems but he – they say it
wasn't dementia, it was ahhmn amnesia, / amnesia –

ROBERT. They said don't call it amnesia, 'You have end-/of-
life memory loss'.

LYDIA. Yes, so that's why –

ROBERT. Well, it makes me laugh!

LYDIA. I just bring –

LYDIA *stands, going to fetch a chair and some biscuits for
the audience as she speaks.*

Well, sit for me as well, I – and I will bring tea for you, tea
or uh – just a tea? What kind of tea? And, uh, we have
biscuits?

ROBERT. I'm not allowed sugar, I might get fat!

LYDIA. I keep a diary, even because it is very important even to know what happened –

ROBERT. Yes for you –

LYDIA. I put in my diary even poo for Robert, because he is constipated. Even here if you go to the bathroom it is written –

ROBERT. Don't lock.

LYDIA. Do not lock. Do not lock, because each / time –

ROBERT. Not each time – once!

LYDIA. There was a lot – I didn't know what to do, I went to the, uh, porter? Saying that Robert's in the bathroom and locked, and he said 'No we cant do,' uh, 'Only ambulance.' And, uh, and Robert was, uh, on the floor, and then, uh, and then –

ROBERT. They said, 'Get up.'

LYDIA. No, uh, uh, they ask you to stay there, to stay. And then he was, uh, so it was so many times that he's just – you have to look at him all the time like, ah, ah, ah, small child, all the time and he, he bashed his head on the bath – he was all in, in blood and then I told him, uh, 'Not to lock, not to lock' and even put NOT-TO-LOCK and then I – (*Mimes trying to open a door.*) and it is locked again! And then I start, 'Why did you lock? Why did you lock?' And he said, 'I forgot!'

ROBERT. How did I get into photography? Oh yes I ha–, I had a studio in over the years in Dover Street in the, uhm, West End and one day somebody phoned me up and said, uhm – (*Cough.*) 'We want you to do a portrait.' I said 'I'm not a portrait photographer' – because… I'm not! They said, 'Well we don't want you because… we want you because we know, uhm, about you – ' and I said 'Well who are you? C'mon, tell me the truth, well, what do you want?' So they said, 'We want you to take a portrait.' So I said, 'I've told you, I've just told you, I'm not a por– ' (*He drifts off into his own world. When he comes back, he's confused to see people watching him.*) Why am I telling you this?

LYDIA (*to the audience*). This biscuits for you, help yourself to as much as you want...

ROBERT. I've lost the train – No I'm kidding so... he said, 'Alright well, uhm, you're safely here now and nobody can hear us. We want you to take a portrait of the Queen.' And I said 'W– ha told you, I'm not a portrait photographer!' – 'All the portrait photographers are connected with the uhm, media, uhm and we want this to be completely secret.' And so I said 'Oh well that makes sense.' And, then I met the Queen! – Where we got to?

LYDIA. I tell you just not to forget there, Robert watch television and then there is occasion – something like that – even if there is, uhhh, he stands – (*Shows us, with her hand on her heart.*) he had a hip replacement and sometimes in such a bad state, he can't get up at all, but he gets up!

ROBERT. I put my hand on there – don't be silly – look I can, that's how I can get up! And I have to be careful – (*He sneakily goes to take a biscuit.*)

LYDIA (*batting his hand away*). It's not for you!

ROBERT. I want one.

LYDIA. Put it back!

ROBERT. See what I have to put up with!

LYDIA. He's pre-diabetic, you have to be careful.

ROBERT. She's Russian she dramatises everything.

Yeah, w, uhh the one on the twenty-pound note is my... if you've got a twenty-pound note, there's the photograph I took!

LYDIA. I told him, 'If you reach one hundred, I will marry you.' He, uh, he asked me long time ago, but I said, 'No, you have to reach first ninety, then ninety-five now one hundred.'

ROBERT. Crazy. When I get to a hundred she'll say 'No, no, no I've always said one hundred and ten.'

*They laugh together.*

*Fade to…*

*A field in a park in the summer. Bristol.*

SARAH *wears a hippie-style, short summer dress.*

*She is sat cross-legged and is playing with buttercups.*

SARAH. I did it all of last summer (*Quick breath.*) jus' while I – while I had, uhm, summer off from studying, uhm, and – it was an amazing experience it actua– it made my summer.

With dementia I've quickly learnt that the best thing you can do is jus' kind of, uhm, hu– to humour them with it a little bit an' cos – which seems dishonest, but you kinda have to go along… I found with Fred particularly, you have to go along with… the lie almost.

His daughter told me, that he, is – uh, he's different now, huh, because of his dementia he's like, he's got quite a different personality an' he's calmer an' more patient than he was when sh– yeah!

Which is really – she said that they didn't get along before h– he had dementia, that he was hu– quite a brute of a man which, to the Fred that I knew, was just complete – the complete opposite.

Cos he was just so tender 'n' patient and I remember one – when, when he was having a bit of an episode of not knowing where he was and freakin' out, uhm, I calmed him down an' – an' he just grabbed my arm, very like – very softly an' just looked at me an' – an' kissed me on the cheek an' said, 'Thank you for th– what you're doing, thank you, I've needed you to be here…'

I'd just had this almost love affair with this man because – an' I'd write in my diary, 'Oh my God, everything he talks about i– we, we're so similar! Like we, we both love coconut cake, we both love tea, he'd talked about the sun in the way that I do – the way it really affects, affects you.'

An' we, we both just sat in the conservatory in this like, green house, just absolutely like gettin' cooked. An' we loved it.

*Newsflash.*

NARRATOR 1. Back in 2010, on the subject of the care system, David Cameron promised that:

DAVID CAMERON. There will be no more of those pointless reorganisations that aim for change but instead bring chaos.

NARRATOR 2. Soon after the election, well-developed plans emerge to completely reorganise the NHS and care system in England through a Health and Social Care Bill.

On 19 January 2011 this Bill is introduced into Parliament. Andrew Lansley, new Health Secretary, says about the Bill:

ANDREW LANSLEY. It is about a process of... modernisation, of reform, of empowerment across the service... right across the NHS we are building the future at the same time as we are maintaining and even improving performance today.

ORDINARY PERSON. So...

NARRATOR. Funding is majorly cut for the NHS and Health and Social Care, as our health-care system instead becomes a market, and subject to European competition law.

NARRATOR 2. Primary Care Trusts, which used to be responsible for ensuring local health systems worked efficiently, which of course included elderly care, are abolished.

NARRATOR. In their place, Clinical Commissioning Groups are set up across England, and run, in theory, by GPs. One NHS official said it is like:

NHS OFFICIAL. Letting the local garage take over BP, or the local corner shop run Sainsbury's.

NARRATOR 2. These groups are also given a much smaller budget with which to do their work, which includes helping organise social care for older people. Their budget is slashed. By thirty-five billion pounds.

*Fade back to…*

*A living room. Christmas.*

PAM *in a reindeer hat.*

PAM. They put her in Tooting. My mum comes from Chelsea, she hasn't seen some of her friends for three years since she's been there. I've been trying to get her out of that care home because, erm, she was dumped there by the council because it was the cheapest one they could find. When I visit her she asks over and over and over to be moved nearer to me.

So I write to the council who the, specially Kensington and Chelsea, uhm, do you know much about the Borough of Kensington? Like, you know they were responsible for Grenfell? They couldn't give a damn about their social, no, council tenants. And they sa–, they um, socially cleanse a lot of people out of the area, um… Well like, with Grenfell, um. That's what they do with the elderly, cos they had erm, they had a care home there. And that was a care home for, that council tenants could go to. But they closed that h'out down and in its place they're building a caviar care home for the family, for the retirement of families of the oligarchs. There's hardly any, erm, erm, council-run care homes any more which of course are properly regulated, but they've all gone private and then so the owners of these homes are running them for profit rather than for care of the people and they would cut corners where they can. To get more profit. So… they won't hire enough staff, because that cuts into their profits, like they do at my mum's home, so… they're just, people are just left in soiled pads for hours, left on toilets, not properly attended to, and, er, and so it, so goes on.

*(Taking her phone out.)* This is how I found her on Saturday, I know it's not nice to look at but look at the state of her legs and her hip. Erm. Her shoes are made for her at the hospital, they, you know, orthopaedic shoes, they're all rolled over

there because the carers don't bother to put her shoes on properly. These bandages put on like that are dangerous, they're dangerous for her circulation, she's in danger of getting a leg ulcer, because of the oedemas and what have you. So, I found that on Saturday and I was so upset I thought, you know, on her eighty-ninth birthday she's got that rubbish!

*Fade out.*

NARRATOR. Rodney Shakespeare, political commentator and Professor of Economics, said:

RODNEY SHAKESPEARE. It's a cynical, dirty game, and it's a betrayal of people who worked their whole lives, who paid into their National Insurance, and now they're being sold down the river.

NARRATOR. In 2012 Andrew Lansley swiftly moved on from his job as Health Minister and has a new job with a private health company. He was replaced. By Jeremy Hunt.

PAULINE *and* ROBERT *enter. They watch.*

JEREMY HUNT. I said when I was offered this job that it was the biggest privilege of my life. I may have been helped by what I suspect was not a long queue of cabinet ministers asking for the same job – (*Laughs.*) but it is an incredible privilege and I am thrilled to be here and I am incredibly grateful to have the chance to work with the NHS over this very, very challenging period in its history.

NARRATOR *goes to talk.*

NARRATOR. What a –

PAULINE *interrupts* NARRATOR.

PAULINE. I think our experience, at this moment in time, makes us very worried.

*She has a face-off with the* NARRATOR.

*Beat.*

*She wins. The* NARRATOR *gives her the stage.*

*Fade to…*

PAULINE *and* ROBIN *are in suits.* PAULINE *is* ROBIN*'s boss.*

I think our experience, at this moment in time, makes us very worried. For the elderly and for the carer, full stop. Unless we start to change our own attitudes. (*Breathes.*) But everything has to be put in a way that's complex, that is complicated, 'Oh it's complicated' – well it isn't. Joe Public could do it, because they know. So when you say, 'What's the hope?' My hope is that they ask Joe Public.

ROBIN. Oh er my work is over at the carers' centre er because there's a, a need for carers to be supported as well. Yeah, it's worked quite well.

PAULINE. Very well.

ROBIN. No it's, it's for unpaid carers, but a lot of people don't know about it. It gives you certain things that you can access which you may not have known about. And some people would still say 'Oh no, no I don't want any help I do it because I really, really care for the person' but what we say is well you can do both, you do care, they are still your husband, your father, your sister, whatever, but, you can also get this help and it's there so, you know, take it up. It doesn't mean you're any less of a person in terms of the loyalty, because you're actually getting help because being a carer can be so emotionally demanding.

PAULINE. The problem that we find –

ROBIN. Ironically –

PAULINE. – is that people have got more issues with the caring service than they have with the person they're caring for and the irony of that is – (*Laughter from both.*) – it just, it doesn't escape you does it really. Ummm. And we try to work with those people about, how to manage that, and it's very difficult to manage a system, or to manage… agencies. A lot of times we've had situations, haven't we?

ROBIN. Yeah.

PAULINE. Where, the quality of care has been so poor, it's put, ironically, a person's life at risk. If you don't give them medication, you've overdosed on the medication, you haven't read the dossette box you've just give 'em a tablet, or you don't write in the book. You know all the things that are in the system that, that are what I'd call safeguards –

ROBIN. Yeah.

PAULINE. They're not done, for a whole range of reasons...

*Fade to...*

*A kitchen.*

KATHY *is peeling potatoes and cutting them into a bowl.*

*She wears brightly coloured clothes.*

KATHY. Well – (*Clears throat.*) they've changed the law now and apparently, apparently you, you – it's all about Health and Safety now, and it's – w – with care now you probably-couldn't-just-get-by-on – you know say, being-a-caring-person you actually-have-to-have-the – you know, relevant qualifications and now you, you have to have, to-work-in-the-care industry, or in anybody's home, you must have an NVQ2 in Health and Social Care, which I do not have... obviously because I'm not working for an agency – (*Breathes.*) erm, you know – (*Smiles.*) it's, it's different. (*Sings.*) *It's different...*

I've said that actually, for an agency, the way – to be honest because I'm s– because I just work for your grandmother a– and I, I, I'm very – I feel I'm very attached to her, I do – I do know that by agency standards they probably would say to me – (*Pause.*) erm, and no– not 'back off' but they would say you have to be a bit more professional rather than sort of, c– cos at the end of the day, I'm not part of the family – (*Clears throat.*) but what I do – but what I do try and do is just be sort of as – just make it as ho– I'm just trying to make it as homely for her as I can rather than like a stranger coming in and – (*Breathes.*) and just sitting down with – just with the same-sort-of-old-routine maybe. I always let her know where Conny i-i-i-is or where – you and Keir aare or who's in the house, that kind of thing, and I just hope that's nice for her because then she knows where everybody is – and knows what everybody's doing.

Erm, but no I-definitely-feel-valued, it's-really-nice, it's-that-feeling-when-you-go-away-and youuu've feel-like-you've-done the best you can do. But no, I would definitely carry on with care work because it's the people that you meet and jsssst – orhhh just, just being part of some – well, loads-of-lovely-people's-lives really, and you've got those little stories that you – (*Breathes.*) will keep forever. I can't imagine not doing it actually if I didn't do caring, I'd do, like voluntary work, something like that. I'd have to do – (*Smiles.*) something.

*Fade back to…*

*A garden in the summer.*

GRAHAM. In my aunt's situation she had eight carers a day, eight different carers a day, now try to negotiate that relationship with a ninety-two-year old woman that is, has partial dementia.

As the cultural and… What was my title? I was the… er… the manager for cultural and creative activities. That was my title.

The attitude then, before I arrived, was erm, 'What do we do? The problem is, what do we do with these people? Once they're up.' Erm. And they, the other problem with – that I tried to address was the – 'What do they want to do? Maybe they don't want to do – we're assuming that these people want to do these things, but – (*Laughs.*) do they want to do these things?' (*Laughs.*)

They are part of the process, you know, do they want to play bingo or not play bingo? I mean there's a lot of assumptions about the way people are cared for – 'They have to go to bed at four o'clock in the afternoon' – well, why do they have to go to bed at four o'clock in the afternoon? (*Laughs*.) You know, they're, they're there to, to be cared for – not, with this regime to take over.

The, the general management idea was, erm, to keep it neat and tidy. Not just physically but that's their kind of mental, emotional – they want it neat and tidy. So if anyone breaks out of that ma– it's like 'AUHHHH!' You know. Panic. Panic. Erm, particularly if a resident goes 'No, fuck off.' Which sometimes… not literally fuck off, just 'No, I'm not doing that' – it's just like 'AUHH, what do you mean you're not doing that? Why don't you want to play bingo? You've got to play bingo! Because it's down on the timetable!' (*Laughs*.) 'I DON'T WANT TO PLAY BINGO.' (*Laughs*.)

*Fade back to…*

*A carers' centre.*

ROBIN. The thing is if you do caring for, in any caring role for like, two years or so, it may even be less than that, your motivation as carer, drops –

PAULINE. Mm, mmm.

ROBIN. Completely drops because you feel as if you're unsupported, it's not going anywhere, ninety-five per cent of the time it's going to get worse rather than better and you get fatigue as a carer, you really do. A lot of people get very, very tired, they get depressed, they get exhausted, they don't feel as if they're having the support – in effect they feel forgotten about.

PAULINE. I think… abandonment, is a really good word, people feel abandoned don't they?

ROBIN. Absolutely –

PAULINE. Or they get a quality of care that's so poor and they think 'Christ Almighty'.

ROBIN. It's about being connected with people and having a sense of a network around you, that you're not on your own. And that's really important.

*Fade back to…*

*A living room. Christmas.*

PAM *is rifling through a large stack of letters.*

PAM. Very few cases get to, erm, be heard by the ombudsman, they dismiss a lot of them. You have to wait about a year anyway, and when you're talking about people in their late eighties, you can't be waiting a year for these sorts of things. And then if they do get a hearing, they nearly always find in favour of the council. It's like an old-boys network with the ombudsman. They look after the local authorities, cos it's all the Tories looking after Tories.

*Fade back to…*

*A hospital waiting room.*

CHARLIE. I just think that sometimes I just get really tired of friends-of-my-mates' suggestions, I'm like, 'Fucking not doing this, you don't get what I'm talking about.' It's a bit mean but sometimes when I hear friends talking I'm like, 'That's not a problem, what are you talking about?! Just cut your hair!' (*Laughs.*) I mean, the – the plus side of it, I mean words are funny, pros and cons and what does that mean? – you're just doing what you're doing – but the plus side of it is, it's made me very athletic about what I do with my time and what I don't do, and who I speak to and who I don't speak to, and I'm quite brutal – like people sort of like, 'Nyaaaehhh' – I can't, I can't, you're not making me laugh, leave it. Or you know, I just don't, oh, just can't, I've only got this much energy and I just can't do it and I'm quite, it's quite – if you're a nice people-pleaser person it's cut that one out of me. (*Laughs.*) Yeah.

*Fade back to…*

*Open-plan sitting room, TV on in the background.*

SHARON. But thinking positively, I took a five-year career break, hoping that I could return, hoping that my mum would be – yeah fine! Maybe that she'd be back up on her feet after two years or something like that. That wasn't the case.

At home it's about ten years now. She was in hospital for three-and-a-half years. She had a... haemorrhage and a stroke.

You want to come?

*Onto the stage comes a hospital bed, a hoist, a wheelchair.*

*Sharon's mother is in the bed.*

*We are now in her bedroom.*

Hi, Mum, this is – (*She asks the audience their name.*)

You say 'hi' to – ? (*Silence.*)

Do you want to go back on your chair? Mum? You wanna go back on your chair? Yeah, I'm coming.

SHARON *talks as she gets her mother up from the bed, using the hoist, into her wheelchair. It's a big move.*

It's just natural innit. It just comes naturally, that's it. Yeah, give me an OBE yeah? (*Laughs.*) I'LL TAKE IT!

You can, you can talk to her. You can talk to her. But it will take time, like, sometimes, not all the time. Sometimes, she'll be fluent like that, it'd just come out of nowhere. But this lady approached me when I was actually coming to visit her in hospital, she goes, she was all, EXCITED, she goes, 'Ooh Sharon, Sharon! Guess what, guess what?' 'What happened, what happened?' I fort it was something serious – she says, 'Your mum spoke.' I go 'Yeah, yeah right, yeah?' She goes 'No, no she did!' You know, 'I'm just going in, with the other trainee colleague, like, erm, and we're just saying "Hello Mary, how're you?" You know... "Fine thanks!" I go, 'My mum don't say "Fine thanks!".' I dunno where she get that from... she doesn't, she'll just say 'Alright,' you know what I'm – 'Fine thanks?' – But I was, I was pleased. I was pleased, I was really, really pleased. I go, 'Say it again.' I go 'Hi, Mum!'(*Beat.*) I ain't get nothing! I ain't get nothing! (*Laughs.*)

It's just, oh gosh. There's a lot I've learnt. Since I've been caring. It's funny cos I did say, like, to myself, like, if anybody came to me and said, 'Sharon, I'm thinking about caring for my friend or my dad or my mum, my sister, my brother,' I'd just look at them – (*Pause*.) and there's no way – it's better for them to make the decision themselves, but I'd say 'If you're gonna go and do it, right? Okay? You better be sure, boy you love them. You love them more than love, care for them' – that's the only way. And who do you love more than anything else in the world? Who? It's gonna be your mother or father. It's gotta be. So, you know, you've got your answer there. You understand me?

*Fade to…*

*Outside a theatre. A round table in the sun.*

EMMA *is glamorously dressed, wearing dark glasses on top of her head, and heels.*

EMMA. I think there is a lot of guilt in being a carer. You know, expectations – not from my mother – amazingly – you know, she's never sort of said – I mean basically, we're like ducks – (*Laughs*.) – paddling away to keep her life – the same. So yeah, there's the guilt. That you're not doing enough, not being there, well – it's about other people's expectations. I think it even comes down to the carers, they think, 'Oh well, you're the daughter.'

And you know, a lot of my anxieties, are not with my mother directly. She doesn't make any demands explicit – implicitly, yes. But – all these people who have all these expectations. And there's one person who keeps saying, 'WHY haven't you sorted out a live-in person? WHY haven't you sorted out – ' Every email, every text, is like, 'What you doing, what you doing, what you doing??' – 'GET OFF MY CASE!' (*Laughs*.)

So people think they're qualified to – yeah, you are judged. But then I guess parents are judged too. But I don't choose it. That's the thing with carers. I don't have children, I'm not married – I chose that, because I like being a career person, I like my freedom. And I've not had anyone depend on me. Well. Until five years ago.

*Fade back to…*

*The carers' centre.*

PAULINE. There's a lot of resentment. So much resentment in some families. Yeah –

ROBIN. I'd been a carer for an aunt in London, and I felt a little bit, sort of, I dunno, embarrassed maybe sometimes saying, 'Oh I'm a carer, for my auntie.' I suppose, on some level, there was something not quite right about being a male, and doing all this, you know? If, if my auntie had had a daughter, if she'd had a niece then probably that daughter or that niece would have done it. Sometimes people fall into that role when it's not necessarily the right thing for them.

PAULINE. But I think that's the same for women, I don't think women are any different / I think there's –

ROBIN. Yeah, of course.

PAULINE. I think there's, when men are the carers, well, cos we've / heard it –

ROBIN. Yeah, yeah –

PAULINE. Where people 'Oh isn't that… ohh / haven't you got a great son.'

ROBIN. Yeah –

PAULINE. 'Ohh, isn't that wonderful!' (*Breathes.*) I think, when men do the caring, I think there's a lot more erm / credit given.

ROBIN. Uhuh.

PAULINE. Ah, sorry / about that.

ROBIN. It's fine –

PAULINE. And I think we do sometimes get that don't / we.

ROBIN. Yeah –

PAULINE. And do people listen to men in services, more than women?

ROBIN (*faintly*). No.

PAULINE. I just think that, I was just wondering / if that –

ROBIN. I don't.

PAULINE. I don't know if that's the case, I'm just saying –

ROBIN. No, no.

PAULINE. I think you were a great carer to Auntie Rosemary.

ROBIN. No but that was, that, that, that's was, that was just a bit of a one-off –

PAULINE. I know, but you were still a great carer. Cos we all loved Auntie Rosemary.

ROBIN. No, well but yes but I could have done better.

PAULINE. Noo, but it's nice that you done a good job.

*She looks at her watch, realises the time. Stands.*

Sorry, anyway, sorry I just, as I said, he was a great carer to Auntie Rosemary… Mmm.

*Fade back to…*

*A hospital waiting room.*

CHARLIE. When Mum came home, I didn't sleep for three months, I didn't have any sleep. Like Mum was up all through the night having these nightmares and I wasn't a very nice person at four in the morning. I mean, everything that I never thought I would say to my mum, I said to her. Like, you know, just, cos you're so tired and you're like, 'Die, die, quickly, die!' Just, aw God forgive me. And my neighbour downstairs is really lovely and she was like 'I thought you were playing your mum lullaby music but then I realised it sounded a bit more like heavy metal like 'GET TO THE FUCKING BED' – (*Laughs.*)

I'm married to my mum, if you like, it feels a bit like that. I mean I feel like a ghost most of the time, the only things you talk about is my mum, and it's like I said to you, I have a life.

*Fade back to…*

*A homely home.*

RUTH *carries on with her make-up.*

RUTH. Obviously you can never go out unless you'd organised it, there was never, 'Right,' spontaneous, 'We'll go out and do this or that.' So you became imprisoned because of somebody who needed your care constantly, and that could be difficult because you, you, you know, you feel – 'Well how long is this gonna go on for?' as well. Because, you're, you're with somebody but they're not them, any more, and you know, you can end up feeling very lonely and you know that there's, no… recovery, there's, there's only one outcome that is ever gonna happen. And that's sad, so you end up mourning them before they've even died, and you know you can, you, you're living with this person who looks like them but isn't them.

When she died, the hole that leaves in your, uhm, whole routine, cos your whole life is rotating round this person, uhm, you feel completely, uhm, displaced. Cos there's no routine, you don't have to stay in, you get this sort of weird sense of freedom that you go out and then you keep thinking, 'I've gotta rush back, I've gotta rush back.'

I went to my church and volunteered for something that I hadn't thought I was going to, which was food bank. And I thought, 'Well that will help me stop feeling so sorry for myself,' cos I was cheesed off by then, cos you do miss that person as well, see? And I went back to school. Yes. I was the oldest pupil there, as you can imagine, and I thought, 'I am not gonna care if they're all twenty and they're all gorgeous and they're all, uh, only just out of school themselves, I'm in my late fifties and I'm gunna go to school and see if I can do maths and English.' Cos when I was sixteen I discovered boys, you see, which was unfortunate, you see. So I went back and I did maths and English and I passed my exams! So I thought, 'Even though I'm ancient, I'm still capable of learning stuff. Even at my age!'

*Beat.*

Society doesn't value carers, because, they're, they are forgotten about. They just say, 'Well you love that person so you'll do it. You've married that person so you'll do it.' And that isn't the answer, that's a cop-out. Because there needs to be provision for everybody. And if I am looking after somebody else, I also have needs and desires and wants that I'm entitled to every bit as much as they are. The people that say, 'Wuw she's your mother, she's your husband, she's your child' are wu-uh, are not doing it. Not in that positions. If they were they would change their mind instantly. They're the forgotten people who do it for the sheer love of doing it and for the fact of doing, just doing it for the right reasons you know…? So no, society doesn't value us, no not at all but that's society's loss, not mine.

*Fade to…*

*A changing room in the NHS.*

STEPH *is in a nurse's uniform. She's about to go on shift.*

STEPH. I mean here's a contradictory, controversial thing to say. Have you ever been to Great Ormond Street? Because they have everything there and they have enormous amounts of resources and enormous amounts of money from various things. And that money is not pumped into elderly care that's a fact. You have to accept it and for various reasons we've made an ethical decision that children are more important and the health of children is more important. That decision's already been made – that isn't an argument in this culture, in this nation. We have, as a nation, let elderly people down. I'm not just speaking as a student nurse, I'm speaking as a young person and as a newly qualified nurse who's about to go into care for elderly people.

*The stage clears.*

NARRATOR. Today, the chaos that Cameron promised to avoid in 2010, is the reality. It is now 2020, twenty-three years since Tony Blair said –

TONY BLAIR. I would say to the country, that previous Labour Governments have done well by Britain's pensioners – always – and we will do well by them again.

NARRATOR. Despite this promise, over the past two decades, no government has followed through on their pledges to take decisive, affirmative action when it comes to improving the care system, and the lives of carers.

NARRATOR 2. But we do have good news. And that's that things can change, if we fight hard enough. That your voice counts. Whilst developing this production, we received this email:

*Fade back to…*

*A living room.*

PAM *reads from an email she's about to send from her laptop.*

PAM. Dear Sam and Zoë.

Thank you for your email, it is good to hear from you again.

Sorry for the late reply – I have been busy preparing notes for a solicitor, sixty-five pages' worth.

I have good news that my mother is now happily moved to a lovely new care home just by Richmond Park. I can visit almost every day. When we get round to a meet-up, I will tell you how I managed it.

I have got a lot more to tell you about but can't until the legal stuff has been completed perhaps in about two months' time, approx. When the legal work has been completed I intend to start knuckling down to completing my mother's book, including everything that has happened since she has been unable to speak for herself due to Alzheimer's – plus the things that I have witnessed regarding lack of care for people in care homes.

Your production company can help make that happen by highlighting what others have witnessed. I would love to go to the production so please keep me posted. The stories need to be told.

Hope to meet up again with you in the not-too-distant future.

Best regards,

Pam.

*The End*.

# HEROES

Isabel Dixon

## ISABEL DIXON

Isabel Dixon is a playwright from the South West, now based in London. She trained on the Royal Court Young Writers Programme, Lyric Hammersmith Writers Group, and Soho Theatre Writers' Lab and Alumni Groups. She was shortlisted for the Old Vic 12 in 2018 and 2019, and was the recipient of the 2019 OffWestEnd.com Adopt a Playwright Award.

Previous credits include *The Plough* (SLAM, now under option for screen); *Frankenstein* (Old Red Lion and The Space); *The Spectacular Starlit Circus* (Watermill Theatre's Federation Project); *Troll* (The Space). Other work has been performed, read and/or developed at theatres including the Old Vic, Young Vic, the Arcola, Rich Mix and BAFTA.

She also works as a dramaturg, facilitator and script reader, and co-founded female-led theatre company Burn Bright Theatre in 2015.

*Heroes* was first performed at VAULT Festival, London, on 18 February 2020. The cast was as follows:

| | |
|---|---|
| JAY | Cole Michaels |
| CAT | Josephine Arden |
| SIAN | Becky Black |
| MARTIN | Paul Brendan |
| JAMIE | Matthew Philip Harris |
| SARAH | Nadia Nadif |
| TOM | TBC |
| *Director* | Lilac Yosiphon |

My thanks first and foremost to the VAULT team: especially Mat Burtcher, Andy George, Bec Martin-Williams and Rhea Heath, as well as the Comms Squad of Josh Morrall, Grace Chapman and Tom Kirk-Shannon. Thanks for having me as part of the Festival family.

Thank you too to my actual family – Mum, Dad, Sam and Noah, as well as the many important people on both sides of our large, complicated but wonderful clan.

This play wouldn't exist without an additional family of people who've given time and love to make it happen: Rebecca Jones and all at SLAM for giving us our first chance to work on the play at the Arcola; Heather Rose, Ellen Stevens and Katherine Timms for their endless encouragement through redrafts and applications; and Nic Connaughton, Ellie Simpson and Jonny Patton at the Pleasance for all of their support. Thank you also to Jules Kelly and the team at Soho Theatre, all at Nick Hern Books, and Mark Brennan at United Agents. And of course, to Josie, Mike, Matt, Becky, Paul, Nadia, Jonny, Tom, Will and everyone who's been a part of the team so far.

Finally, thank you to Lilac – whose endless support, love and passion has made this all happen. Here's to the families we make when we make things.

*I.D.*

## Characters

*A-Side: 1991*

JAMIE, *fifteen*
MARTIN, *forty-two*
SIAN, *nineteen*
TOM, *fifteen*

*B-Side: 2016*

JAY, *forty*
MARTIN, *sixty-seven*
SIAN, *forty-four*
SARAH, *forty*
CAT, *thirty-six*

## Time

Sometimes the action takes place in 1991.

Sometimes the action takes place in 2016.

Sometimes the action takes place in both years at the same time.

## Note on Casting

Characters who appear in both 1991 and 2016 can be played by
the same actors throughout, reducing the cast size. However,
JAY and JAMIE should always be played by different actors.

## Note on Text

/ marks a sentence interrupted by the next character talking over.

– marks a line or thought cut short.

… marks a sentence that trails off.

## Scene One

*A family living room, somewhere in suburbia, in 1991.*

*A living room, in a smartish but comfortable flat in London, in 2016.*

*Both of these spaces exist together.*

*As the audience enter, we see the characters in both timeframes interacting with the world around them.*

*There are cards and envelopes across the set – we are celebrating something in both years.*

*In 2016,* CAT, *mid-thirties and very pregnant, puts a cup of tea down and sits on the sofa, silently reading through a pile of cards. Somewhere in the background water is running.*

*In 1991,* MARTIN, *late thirties, watches fifteen-year-old* JAMIE *as he opens a present. It's a record player.* JAMIE *lifts the lid.*

MARTIN. Be gentle with it.

JAMIE. I am.

MARTIN. I mean it. I don't want to see it get broken.

JAMIE. You don't have to give it to me.

MARTIN. I want to.

JAMIE. If you're worried I'll break it.

MARTIN. I know you won't. I'm just being silly.

*Beat.*

I got that for my fifteenth birthday.

JAMIE. Nan got me a Walkman.

MARTIN. Not the same. Not as good.

JAMIE. Don't tell her that.

MARTIN. The thing about a record is, it sounds best when you listen to the whole thing. Without stopping. Start to end, all in the right order, like a story. None of this jumping about or rewinding or skipping to the good bits.

JAMIE. What's wrong with skipping to the good bits?

MARTIN. You miss out on stuff. Details.

*Beat.*

Where's your mum put the iron?

JAMIE. Downstairs cupboard.

*MARTIN exits just offstage.*

*In 2016, JAY, forty, enters, dressed in a bathrobe. CAT doesn't look up.*

JAY. Have you seen the iron?

*Beat.*

Cat?

CAT. It's in a box in the bedroom.

JAY. Which one?

CAT. Don't know.

JAY. I can't go to work with my shirts all crumpled up, can I?

CAT. Yeah you can. You've just moved house.

JAY. To Zone 4, not a cave.

CAT. Try the one by the mirror with all the bathroom bits in.

*JAY exits. JAMIE puts a record on. 'Space Oddity' by David Bowie starts to play.*

JAMIE. I haven't got any records.

MARTIN (*off*). You can keep that one.

JAMIE. Nah. No. It's alright.

MARTIN (*off*). It's part of the present.

JAMIE. It's your favourite.

MARTIN *re-enters, iron in hand*.

MARTIN. Can't go into school with a crumpled shirt, can I?

JAMIE. Nobody's going to care.

MARTIN. Means I can't tell your year off for not looking smart.

JAMIE. Who's Major Tom?

MARTIN. What?

JAMIE. Major Tom. On the record.

MARTIN. Oh, right. He's an astronaut. He's not real.

*Beat.*

I thought, this would be good for before you go to see him.

JAMIE. Yeah. Thanks.

MARTIN. We could both go. I got you two tickets.

JAMIE. Oh.

MARTIN. What?

JAMIE. I thought. I asked / Tom –

MARTIN. Oh, that's fine. No, that's alright.

JAMIE. Sorry.

MARTIN. No point going with an old bugger like me. I'll just show you up.

JAMIE. I can tell him you're coming instead.

MARTIN. Another time. Eh?

JAMIE. Sorry.

MARTIN. Stop saying sorry. It's fine.

*Beat*. MARTIN *picks up the record sleeve*.

I'll have to get you some more of these. Dig out my stash in the attic. Don't tell your mum, she'll be on at me for not giving Sian a player as well.

MARTIN *picks up the wrapping paper on the floor and takes it offstage.*

JAY *re-enters, iron in hand.*

JAY. How many cards is that, now?

CAT. We got five more this morning.

JAY. I don't know where we're going to put them all.

CAT. Ha. Wait till Sprog arrives. People send you loads of crap when you have a baby.

JAY. Babies don't need cards.

CAT. They send us the cards, you muppet.

*He picks up a card, looks at it briefly, sets it back down.*

JAY. Maybe I should take Friday off. Try and get us properly unpacked before the / weekend.

CAT. Were you crying in the shower?

*Beat. She puts her tea down and waits.*

Jay?

JAY. No.

CAT *turns off the radio – 'Space Oddity' cuts out, as if it's been playing in 2016 and not on* JAMIE*'s player in 1991.*

CAT. Yes, you were.

JAY. Probably next door.

CAT. Next door? She's in her eighties. Give me a break.

*Beat.*

I thought I was meant to be the hormonal one.

Talk to me.

JAY*'s silent. Meanwhile,* JAMIE *is still examining the record player.*

JAMIE. Sian doesn't care. She's not into records.

MARTIN. She likes different things. That's what I keep explaining to your mum – you take after me.

JAMIE. You think?

MARTIN. Yeah.

JAY. I don't know.

CAT. You don't know why you were crying?

*Beat.*

JAY. Did you hear David Bowie died?

CAT. What?

JAY. Cancer. He died, he had cancer.

CAT. I know that, it was on the radio. Don't change the subject.

JAY. It's weird, isn't it?

CAT. We're having a conversation, Jay.

JAY. No, I know –

CAT. What, you've been crying in the shower because David
    Bowie died?

*Beat. CAT sighs.*

JAY. I'm fine. Cat? I'm fine. Seriously.

CAT. I've never seen you cry. Ever.

JAY. No. It's just – when someone you've looked up to, you
    know. And cancer, as well. That's sort of so… final, isn't it.

*Beat.*

CAT. Oh, God. Jay.

JAY. No, no I know what you're about / to say –

CAT. Cancer. Of course.

JAY. No, no –

CAT. Keep forgetting about your mum. Not because she's
    forgettable – just, I never met her.

JAY. It's nothing. No big deal.

CAT. Of course it's a big deal.

JAY. It's just a… thing, is all. A childhood memory. It's nothing.

*Silence. She stands up and hugs him. He doesn't hug her back.*

MARTIN *watches* JAMIE *with the player.*

MARTIN. He went all Ziggy Stardust after this. Then Aladdin Sane, then the Thin White Duke when he was just living on red peppers and milk and cocaine. A different person all the time.

JAMIE. Why would you do that?

MARTIN. What do you mean?

JAMIE. He's David Bowie. Everyone loves David Bowie.

MARTIN *shrugs.*

MARTIN. Everyone wants to do that, don't they? Stop being you for a bit, and be someone else. Somebody different.

JAMIE. I don't.

MARTIN. Don't you?

JAMIE *shakes his head.*

That's cos you're fine as you are, I expect.

CAT. Sorry.

JAY. Don't do that. It's not you, okay?

*Beat.* CAT *kisses him.*

CAT. Sorry.

JAY. Stop saying sorry.

CAT. I am though. I am sorry. I'm a bag of hormones. I feel like a beached whale. I keep having dreams where you leave me, or you disappear, I wake up and I'm by myself – and it's made me a bit –

JAY. Where I leave you?

CAT. Just – yeah, it's probably pre-birth anxiety / it's no big –

JAY. Why would I do that?

CAT. You wouldn't.

JAY. That's insane.

CAT. Yeah, I know.

*Beat. He looks at her.*

JAMIE. Why would you want to? Be someone else.

MARTIN. I don't know. Be cool, wouldn't it, to be a rockstar instead of a PE teacher for a bit?

JAMIE. Tell that to people at school. They already think you're a rockstar.

MARTIN. What about you?

JAMIE. I dunno. You're my dad, aren't you?

CAT. I just worry, sometimes, that you don't seem that excited. About being a dad.

MARTIN *smiles*.

JAMIE. You're just my dad.

JAY. I am excited.

CAT. Well, it wasn't exactly planned –

JAY. It was a surprise. A good surprise. Really.

CAT. I just –

I wish you wouldn't get so freaked out. When she kicks and stuff. It's like you get scared remembering she's real, that she's coming –

JAY *kisses her*.

JAY. You're going to have to stop calling her Sprog when she gets here.

CAT. Help me pick a name then.

*Beat.*

JAY. Everything's fine.

CAT. I know.

JAY. Sorry for crying in the shower.

CAT. Crying over Bowie. You soft git.

JAY. Yeah, right.

CAT. You'd better cry at the birth now, or I'll be proper offended.

*Beat.* JAY *picks up her empty mug.*

MARTIN. Right. School. Come on.

CAT. Who's Martin?

JAMIE *grabs his bag.* MARTIN *picks up his keys. They exit.*

JAY. What?

CAT. Martin. Who's Martin?

JAY. I don't know.

CAT. We've got a card from him, look. A congratulations card for the move – and about you becoming a dad… He doesn't mention me.

JAY. Could be a new neighbour, or –

CAT. He calls you Jamie. Nobody calls you Jamie. Jamie is the you in your mum's old school photos with your gangly limbs and weird haircut. It's got to be someone who knows you – it's all about you, look –

JAY. Probably a friend of Mum's, or something.

CAT. Why would he send you a card if he was a friend of your mum's?

JAY. I don't know, Cat.

*It's a little too forceful. She falls silent.*

Forget about it. Chuck it in the bin. We've got too many anyway.

CAT. Alright.

*Silence. She stands up and picks up her bag.*

I've got to go.

JAY. I wish you weren't still going in.

CAT. It's two more weeks.

JAY. Right.

*She puts one hand on her stomach.*

CAT. She's kicking a bit, today. She doesn't like it when we bicker.

JAY. We're not bickering.

CAT. Okay.

*Beat.*

We'll see you later, then.

*She waits, as if she's waiting for him to kiss her or hug her, or even to say goodbye – but after a moment, it's clear that he's not going to. CAT puts her bag over her shoulder and leaves. The front door slams.*

*JAY waits until he hears the door and looks through the cards, tearing open envelopes, barely stopping to read each one before he casts it aside on the floor.*

### Scene Two

*2016, later the same day. A coffee shop, somewhere in East London. Not trendy – a greasy spoon. 'Life on Mars' plays tinnily over a run-down PA system.*

*JAY sits at a table, tearing open sugar packets and pouring the contents into a neat pile. Distracting himself.*

*SIAN, early forties, smart suit, enters. JAY doesn't look up as SIAN sits down.*

*Beat.*

SIAN. Stop that.

*He looks at her and sweeps the sugar into a napkin.*

Have some respect for the waiting staff. They don't want to be clearing up your mess, do they? Not on nine quid an hour.

*Beat.*

I've got half an hour for lunch, Jamie, are you actually going to talk to me?

JAY. Nobody calls me that any more. You know that.

SIAN. If we're going to sit here and fuck about with what you prefer to be called now, I'll leave and go to Pret for a sandwich instead.

*Beat.*

How's Catherine?

JAY. She's fine.

SIAN. And the baby?

JAY. It's all fine.

SIAN. Am I going to get to meet her at some point? Ever?

*Beat.*

I'll take that as a no.

*Beat.*

So what can I do for you?

JAY. We got a card. From Dad.

SIAN. Ah.

JAY. How did he get my address?

SIAN. I gave it to him.

*Beat.*

JAY. Fuck's sake, Sian. Are you serious?

SIAN. He's dying, Jamie.

*Silence.*

Cancer. Like Mum. But in his liver. It's bad.

*Silence.* JAY *stares at her. Then he continues pouring the sugar.*

JAY. Good.

SIAN. You don't mean that. That's just horrible. That isn't you.

*Beat.*

JAY. You had no right.

SIAN. Are you going to answer it? The letter?

JAY. No. He'll keep writing though, won't he? I mean...

*Beat.*

SIAN. Maybe he wants to tell you he's sorry.

JAY. Do you think he's told Sarah Reagan's mum he's sorry?

SIAN. No.

*Beat.*

JAY. I'm not going to see him.

SIAN. Fine. That's your choice. I just wanted you to have a choice, that's all.

JAY. You're judging me for it, though.

SIAN. I'm not. Do whatever works for you.

JAY. I wish he'd never gotten out. He shouldn't have gotten out.

SIAN. Well, he did. Years ago, actually, and you didn't care then either if you remember –

JAY. Did you see him?

*Beat.*

You said you weren't going to. Never again, you said.

SIAN. Mum's gone, Jay, he's all we've got / left.

JAY. So, what, you've changed your mind now?

SIAN. Yes, sort of. I have spoken to him, yeah. A couple of times, only in the last few months.

JAY. In person.

SIAN. Yes.

JAY. You said.

SIAN. I know.

JAY. So. Why?

SIAN. Because nobody else does.

*Silence. She tries, very tentatively, to take his hand. He pulls it away.*

Alright, fine. Be angry about it then, I don't care.

JAY. What he did –

SIAN. What he did won't go away, and that's the worst part, Jay. We just sit there, when I see him. With this silence echoing. All the things we want to say but can't.

*Beat.*

I can't hug him either. Even though he's just this bag of bones in a polo shirt and joggers, like a baby bird or something. It turns me cold.

*Beat.*

Do you remember when I ruined his cassette collection?

JAY. No.

SIAN. Yes, you do. I was fourteen, remember? So you'd have been in primary school still. He wouldn't let me go to Mark Wilson's party because he found fags in my rucksack. So I got all his cassettes – got every single one out of the plastic tape-deck tower – and I pulled the tape out of them. Left them all in a big heap of snaky ribbons. And when he saw them, he made me sit at the table with a pencil and wind each one back in till my knuckles clicked. Couldn't do that now, could you?

JAY. Do you reckon they let you have cassettes in prison?

*She ignores him.*

SIAN. He'd have never done that to you, you fucking golden
     boy.

JAY. That why you gave him my address? To punish me?

SIAN. Grow up, Jamie. Course I didn't.

     *Beat.*

     You might regret it, if you don't. It won't be long.

JAY. No, I won't.

     *Beat.*

SIAN. Did you hear David Bowie died?

JAY. Yeah.

SIAN. Dad's favourite.

JAY. Was he?

SIAN. You know he was.

JAY. Don't remember.

SIAN. You don't expect some people to die, do you? They're
     just sort of – You think they'll go on and on.

     *Beat.*

     I thought he might've hit me. When he saw the tapes. All this
     fucking music spilling out onto the floor. And just this white-
     hot rage, him balling up his fists – but I remember thinking,
     well, teachers can't hit their own kids, can they? Can you
     imagine what people would say?

     *Beat. JAY doesn't react. She stands up slowly, gathering her
     belongings.*

     Take care of yourself, Jamie.

**Scene Three**

*10 November 1991.*

JAMIE*'s bedroom. Scruffy, clothes everywhere, cassettes stacked up by the bed. The record player is on the floor.*

TOM, *also fifteen, dog-eared school uniform, sits on the floor rolling a cigarette.* JAMIE *flicks through a magazine.*

JAMIE. You better not let my mum and dad see you with that.

TOM *ignores him, licking the Rizla.*

Can you do me one?

TOM. I'll do it when we get to the station.

JAMIE. You've brought other clothes, yeah?

TOM. Course.

JAMIE. Okay.

TOM. Not going to go Brixton in my school uniform, am I?

*Beat.*

JAMIE. You know who else likes Bowie.

TOM. Don't.

JAMIE. Sarah Reagan.

TOM. Fuck off, Jamie.

JAMIE. You fancy her.

TOM. No, I don't.

JAMIE. You keep perving over her in maths. You go proper glazed behind the eyes –

TOM. I'm fucking concentrating, aren't I. On the maths.

JAMIE. I don't blame you. She's fit.

TOM. You're being a dick.

JAMIE. Sorry.

*Beat.*

You should ask her out.

TOM. No.

JAMIE. Why not?

>TOM *shakes his head and focuses intently on rolling another cigarette.*

She's pretty.

TOM. I know.

JAMIE. So ask her out.

TOM. I never speak to her though, do I?

JAMIE. Worst thing she can say is no.

TOM. You wouldn't do it, if you were me.

JAMIE. I would.

TOM. When was the last time you asked anybody out?

JAMIE. I'm just / saying –

TOM. Well don't / say –

JAMIE. Nobody's going to die just because you want to go out with someone.

TOM. Can you drop it?

>*Beat.*

JAMIE. Anyway, if you wank too much over her you'll go blind.

TOM. I mean it, Jamie. You're being a cunt. I'm not going to come Brixton with you if you don't fuck off.

>*Beat.*

JAMIE. You'll miss out on Bowie then.

>*Beat.*

TOM. Yeah, well.

JAMIE. So you can't not come.

>*Beat.*

If you don't ask her out, I'll do it / for you –

TOM. I swear to fucking / God –

JAMIE. Okay, okay, fucking hell.

TOM*'s up on his feet, angry and mortified. Silence.*

TOM. Should have asked your dad to go with you.

JAMIE. It's my birthday present. I want you to come.

*Beat.* TOM *is slightly calmer.*

TOM. I can't do the pictures any more though.

JAMIE. What do you mean, you can't?

TOM. Ran out of film and I've got no money.

JAMIE. Fuck's sake – I'd have lent you money if you'd asked –

*Beat.*

Proper music journos have pictures.

TOM. Well, proper photographers have cameras. And film.

JAMIE. We could borrow my dad's.

TOM. What? No, we couldn't.

JAMIE. It's fine.

TOM. What if it gets broken? Or stolen – it's Brixton, remember –

JAMIE. It's not that good a camera.

TOM. We should ask first.

JAMIE. If we ask he'll say no.

TOM. Right, well, that really makes me want to take it, so –

JAMIE. Look. It's not a big deal, alright, we'll just replace the film we use. You can take it, get them developed, I'll buy another roll – he won't even realise they're gone.

TOM. But –

JAMIE. Wait here.

JAMIE *disappears, leaving* TOM *standing awkwardly, twisting the freshly rolled cigarette between his fingers.* JAMIE *reappears moments later with a manual Canon camera inside a case.*

See? It's just sitting in the games cupboard. I bet he hasn't picked it up in months.

TOM *unzips the case.*

TOM. There's pictures on this roll already.

JAMIE. So?

TOM. So – he'll know if you put a fresh one in.

JAMIE. He's probably forgotten they're even there. I'll just sneak them in with the last round of holiday pictures, he'll never know.

TOM *isn't sure.* JAMIE *can see he's about to make excuses.*

JAMIE. Stop being scared of him just because he's a teacher.

TOM. I'm not.

JAMIE. You're obsessed with him liking you. Everyone is.

TOM. He's not like other teachers, though, is he? He's cool.

JAMIE. He's just my dad.

TOM, Yeah, but –

JAMIE. Look. It's Bowie. You can't miss out on getting pictures of Bowie.

TOM*'s on the fence.* JAMIE *picks up a cassette, shoves it in the player, clicks play. 'Rebel Rebel' gently starts to play.*

It's Bowie, Tom.

TOM. Alright. But if he finds out –

JAMIE. Then it's on me. Okay? But he won't. Nobody's going to find out.

*He pulls the roll-up out of* TOM*'s hand and tucks it behind his ear. The song continues playing.*

## Scene Four

*2016. One week later. A bland room, featureless, medical – in a hospital or a hospice.*

MARTIN, *in his late sixties, frail and with a beanie hat covering a bald head, sits in an armchair. He's got a sudoku book on his lap.*

JAY *stands several feet from him.*

MARTIN. Look at you.

> *Silence.* JAY *doesn't respond.*

> I'm glad you came.

> *Silence.*

> You look like your mother these days, Jamie. Not much of me in there now.

JAY. Jay. Not Jamie.

MARTIN. That's right. Sian said.

JAY. Nobody's called me Jamie in years.

MARTIN. Old habits. Sorry.

> *Silence.*

> Do you want to sit down?

JAY. No.

MARTIN. You'd be more comfortable.

JAY. No, I won't.

> *Beat.*

> Why did you send me a card?

MARTIN. I thought it was worth trying. Worth saying something.

JAY. I don't want to hear from you. I thought I'd made that clear –

MARTIN. It's been twenty-odd years since I've last seen you, mate.

JAY. Twenty-five / actually –

MARTIN. And given the circumstances –

JAY. The circumstances don't change anything.

MARTIN. You're going to be a dad.

JAY. And?

MARTIN. And I wanted –

JAY. You're coming nowhere near my child.

*Beat.*

MARTIN. Okay.

JAY. You didn't send a card when Mum died, did you?

MARTIN. Well. No. It didn't seem / appropriate –

JAY. You selfish fuck.

*Beat.*

MARTIN. I hadn't seen her in years either, Jamie. We were divorced.

JAY. Because of you.

MARTIN. Because of me.

*Beat.*

It wouldn't have made things better. Sending a condolence card from prison – it's not like you wanted to speak to me.

JAY. It's not about you.

*Beat.*

Sian had to hold everything together. Plan the funeral, contact all the relatives. And even before that – be there when she was sick, doing chemo…

MARTIN. Sian didn't want to speak to me then either.

JAY. But we're supposed to drop everything for you? Now it's your turn to be ill?

MARTIN. No. You don't have to do anything you don't want to do.

*Beat.*

What would you do, if you knew you were dying?

JAY *shrugs.*

Normal people – even the ones who didn't fuck up like I did – they have a lot of regrets on their deathbed. I was reading about it the other day. 'I wish I'd spent more time with my family' – that's at the top. 'I wish I'd travelled more.'

JAY. If your biggest regret is that you didn't travel more, you've got bigger fucking problems / than cancer –

MARTIN. It's not.

JAY. Good.

*Beat.*

Things don't just get brushed under the carpet now you're…

*Beat.*

MARTIN. I cried every night for the first six months. When I first went in.

*Beat.*

It was like being eaten from the inside out. Everything I'd done. You, Sian, your mum. And –

JAY. No. Don't say it.

MARTIN. Okay.

JAY. I don't want to talk about this.

MARTIN. Okay.

*Silence.*

You go sort of numb, after a while. Even now. With this. I'm not – being sick, it doesn't scare me. It just is. It's what's happened. No changing it. You shut your brain off, you know?

*Silence.*

Sian got me the hat. It's itchy.

*Silence.*

JAY. I'm going.

MARTIN. Alright. See you, then.

*Beat.*

You can come back. If you want.

JAY. I don't want.

MARTIN. If you need to.

*Silence.*

If you change your mind, Jamie.


**Scene Five**

*Two living rooms, one in 1991, one in 2016.*

*In 2016,* CAT *is sitting on the sofa, a single picture on the coffee table in front of her.*

*In 1991, the family living room is a mess. It's been searched, thoroughly. Stacks of items sit piled up, riffled through.*

SIAN, *now nineteen, is smoking and trying to stack the debris.* JAMIE *sits on the sofa.*

SIAN. They should clear up after themselves. If they ransack your fucking house, then that should be…

JAMIE. Mum doesn't like smoking indoors.

SIAN. Mum doesn't like me smoking full stop.

CAT *picks up her phone and tries to make a call. It rings out. She hangs up and, frustrated, sits back on the sofa.*

JAMIE. Why are you back?

SIAN. I'm not going to sit in Bristol with all this going on, am I?

JAMIE. I can take care of it.

SIAN. You're fifteen, Jamie.

*She stubs out the cigarette.*

JAMIE. She's lying. You know that, don't you?

*SIAN is silent. She carries on clearing up.*

*In 2016 a key grinds in the lock. JAY enters.*

JAY (*off*). I'm home.

*Silence.*

Cat?

JAMIE. Sian?

CAT. I'm in here.

SIAN. We just have to see what happens, yeah?

JAMIE. Loads of girls in our year fancy Dad. It's a joke –
people always joke about it.

SIAN. This isn't a joke, Jamie. Jesus. What is wrong with you?

*JAY enters.*

JAY. What's wrong with you?

CAT. What do you mean, what's wrong with me?

*She hands him the picture. She exits. JAY looks at it and
realises – he's fucked up.*

JAMIE. What happens now?

SIAN. Depends if they found anything else, I think.

JAMIE. Where's Mum?

*Beat.*

JAY. Shit. Cat –

CAT (*off*). You forgot.

JAY. No.

CAT (*off*). What, you didn't forget? You just chose not to come?

*She re-enters and stares at him.*

SIAN. Mum's in her room. Just leave her for a bit, yeah?

JAY. No – I'm sorry – I did. Forget I mean.

JAMIE. There won't be anything else. Once we clear this up – it'll all be fine.

SIAN. You don't know that, Jamie.

JAMIE. It's a mistake.

SIAN *looks at him, trying to find the right words.*

JAY. It was a mistake. An accident.

CAT. And you keep telling me you're fine with this – that you want to be a dad –

JAY. I do.

CAT. I asked you so many times. You know I hate going on my own, I fucking hate hospitals.

JAY. I just – forgot.

CAT. You can't forget this stuff. You just can't. That's part of being an adult.

JAY *is silent. He sits down on the sofa.*

JAMIE. Why do you keep staring at me like that?

SIAN. Nobody's staring.

*Beat.*

You know they wouldn't search the house without…
reasons, Jamie. You know that, right?

JAMIE. This happens all the time, though. People lying about teachers –

SIAN. Why are you so sure she's lying?

JAMIE. Because it's Dad. Isn't it?

CAT. What is going on with you? Seriously?

JAY. Nothing's going on. I got held up at work, / it was busy, it slipped my mind –

CAT. Yeah. I called your work. You weren't there.

*Silence.*

If you're cheating on me, you need to tell me / now. Now.

JAY. Of course I'm not –

CAT. Because this doesn't look great. You know that, right?

JAMIE. It's just pictures. Anyone could have taken them.

*JAY picks up the scan.*

JAY. Is she okay?

CAT. I just wanted you there. When we saw her again.

SIAN. It's Dad's camera.

JAY. I took the afternoon off and went to see Mum. Mum's grave, I mean.

*Silence.*

CAT. You should have called me.

JAY. I know.

CAT. I'd have come with you.

JAY. I needed to be by myself.

*Beat. JAMIE sits down on the sofa.*

CAT. I want you to promise me.

JAY. I promise.

CAT. That you're not hiding / anything. That if anything was going on –

JAY. I forgot. And I'm so sorry. It won't happen again.

This is my fault, okay? I'm an idiot.

CAT *sighs.*

JAMIE. Do you think this is my fault?

*Beat.*

Sian?

SIAN. What do you mean?

JAMIE. I gave Tom the camera.

SIAN. It's not your fault.

*Silence. Both pairs sit next to each other on the sofa.*

## Scene Six

*1991. The living room.* JAMIE *is standing in the doorway, carrying a bucket of soapy water and a sponge.*

TOM *sits on the sofa with* SIAN. *He's been crying. The room is still a mess.*

JAMIE. What's he doing here?

*Beat.*

SIAN. Tom's come round to talk to you.

JAMIE. I don't want to.

SIAN. He's your friend, Jamie –

JAMIE. Piss off.

TOM. I can help you. With that.

JAMIE. You can help me? Why do you think people are spraying the side of our house?

SIAN. Jamie.

TOM. I thought I was doing the right thing –

JAMIE. You were my best friend.

TOM. There were photos of her, Jamie. I had to tell someone.

JAMIE. Do you still think you've done the right thing?

*Beat.*

It's your fault, you know. That / she's –

SIAN. Don't say things like that, fucking hell –

JAMIE. I bet you held on to the pictures, didn't you?

TOM. No, of course I didn't – it's not right, / Jamie –

JAMIE. People wouldn't have known, would they, if you hadn't said anything.

TOM. I didn't make your dad –

JAMIE. You could have come to me / or…

TOM. I went to my parents, didn't I. I didn't know what to do. And they called the police.

*Beat.*

JAMIE. This isn't the first time someone's painted the house, or chucked a brick through the window.

*Beat.*

And where were you? It's been weeks.

TOM. I knew you'd be angry. That's why I didn't… Before.

*Silence.* JAMIE *sits on the floor with his head in his hands.* SIAN *takes the bucket.*

SIAN. I'm going to go and clean it up. Alright? Just – stay here.

*She exits.*

JAMIE. Do you think I'm like him?

TOM. What do you mean? Like your dad?

JAMIE. I don't know what I mean any more.

*Beat.*

TOM. I would've…

It wasn't to do with me liking her. You know that? I wasn't trying to get your dad into trouble / because of that –

JAMIE. I know.

TOM. I didn't know what to do, Jamie.

TOM *starts to cry.*

JAMIE. I told everyone she was lying. Everyone.

*Silence.*

TOM. Do you hate me?

*Silence.*

JAMIE. Yeah.

*Silence.*

I never want to fucking see you again.

## Scene Seven

CAT *and* JAY*'s living room. She's sitting on the floor, cross-legged, with a pile of letters.*

*She's been crying. A suitcase, packed, sits next to her.*

JAY *stands by the door staring at her, horrified.*

CAT. He's your dad.

JAY. Where did you get those?

CAT. This… Martin. The one you said was a friend of your mum's –

JAY. Did you go through my stuff?

CAT. All these. Fuck.

*Beat.*

How long's this been going on?

JAY. A couple of months. That's all. Sian gave him my address, that's why we got that card. I've seen him, twice, maybe three times –

CAT. You told me your dad was dead. Heart attack, you were so young you can barely remember, that's what you said.

*Beat.*

JAY. I know.

*Beat.*

CAT. We're about to have a baby. Everything I thought I knew about you…

JAY. It's / not –

CAT. You lied to me.

JAY. I'm sorry.

*Silence.*

CAT. How long have you known he's still alive? Or – no, I'm so stupid. You've always known, haven't you? You've lied since the start.

JAY. No / not exactly.

CAT. You have.

*Silence.*

I kept wondering – why you weren't more excited. I thought it was my fault. I thought you weren't ready – that this was all unplanned and you wouldn't have chosen to have a baby, not right now.

*Beat.*

But then I'd tell myself, well it makes sense, doesn't it? Because you don't have your parents any more – so, of course it's going to be weird for you. Hard for you. I can't imagine not getting to see my mum and dad become grandparents…

JAY. It's not – of course I want to be a dad. I do.

*Beat.*

CAT. I've packed you a bag. I think you need to leave for a bit.

JAY. Please don't say that.

CAT. I don't know what else to do, Jay.

JAY. He's been dead, to me. Cat? Do you understand? / As far as I was concerned – it was like he didn't exist –

CAT. No, of course I don't fucking understand. If someone's dead, they're dead, if they're not then they're alive. That's how it works.

*Beat.*

You told me you loved your dad. He was your hero, you said.

JAY. He was. Before.

CAT. So why would you / tell me –

JAY. Because it was easier.

*Beat.*

My dad did something. When I was a teenager. He did something bad, and he went to prison. And he was in prison for a long time. And I never saw him again. I mean, until now.

CAT. What did he do?

JAY. He's dying. I'm seeing him because… I don't know. Sian wants me to, and I need to make this easier for her. Or something. I have things I need to say –

CAT. What did he do?

*Silence.*

JAY. My dad was a teacher, at the school I was at. He was everyone's favourite teacher. Everyone loved him. Everyone used to say I was so lucky, that he was my dad. And he…

*Beat.*

When I was fifteen, he slept with a girl in my year. Had a relationship with her, sort of. He knew she was fifteen. And he got found out and… so. He went to prison.

*Beat.*

The girl – the girl he slept with. We grew up in a small town, so everyone knew about it. And it wasn't – I mean, it was worse back then anyway, but he was married, and she was underage and it was all over the papers. And people talked. I remember at the time, what it was like for us, me and Sian and Mum, but it was worse for her. And even worse than that, was Dad saying he didn't do anything. Said she was lying – after he told her he loved her, made her feel...

*Beat.*

So before Dad got sentenced proper – when they were going to make her testify... she. Took some pills. She nearly died. And there were hospitals and police and people searching our house and then... she moved away. Dad went to prison.

CAT. Jesus Christ.

*Silence.*

JAY. That's it. That's the whole story.

*Silence. She tentatively puts a hand out to him.*

CAT. I can understand why you hate him for what he did. But Jay –

JAY. No, no – it's not that.

*Silence. He's trying to find the words.*

He said he didn't do it. When he got arrested. When they came to our house and went through everything, all the cupboards and sock drawers. When they took me and Sian off and sat us down with social workers to ask if he'd ever – and I said no, of course not, I said Sarah Reagan was lying. Because she had to be. And Dad said she was – said it was all a mistake. I told everyone that she lied. Joined in when everyone made fun of her. Because it would have been me otherwise, and that was better than getting told your dad's a paedo in the school corridors, right?

*Beat.*

A schoolgirl crush that got out of control – that's what he said to Mum, and I believed him. Even when they found pictures, he told me they weren't his, and I still believed it. I even got up in court and said it. That it was all lies. And then – just at the last minute. When she tried to. You know. He sort of... crumbled. Collapsed in on himself. And he told me it was all true, and it was all his fault.

*Beat.*

And I sort of just – I don't know, held him, this awkward
teenager, in this waiting room – in prison, they're like these
rooms with painted walls and the tables you have at school,
and plastic chairs – and I just. I sat there and I held him
while he cried. Like a baby. Like he couldn't stop. And
everything about it made my skin crawl. And I couldn't...

*Beat.*

I didn't see him again, after that.

CAT. You were a kid.

JAY. I was fifteen.

CAT. That's nothing. You were a child. So was she. What were
you meant to do?

*She tries to touch his arm again and he pushes her off.*

Nobody could blame you. I don't blame you.

JAY. What if I'm like him?

CAT. Of course you're not.

JAY. How do you know that?

*Beat.*

I mean, I believed him, didn't I? So did Mum – Sian –

CAT. Because I know you.

JAY. I've lied to you all this time, you / didn't –

CAT. That's different.

JAY. Is it?

*Silence.*

I was so like him. Everyone used to say it. Like father, like
son.

CAT. Is that why you're so scared / about the baby?

JAY. What if I hurt it? Or –

CAT. Don't say that. Don't ever say that. Of course you won't.

JAY. How do you know that? Sarah – the girl – she was younger than Sian was. His own daughter.

CAT. I promise you, you're not going to turn into him.

JAY. But you don't know that. Not for certain. Neither do I.

*Beat.*

I used to – when I was at university. I couldn't go near girls, for ages. I'd come close and then I'd get too scared, like there was something under the surface and it'd just take the smallest push to tip me under. Like there was a black hole inside me, sewn up, waiting to burst its stitches.

*Beat.*

I always said, I don't want kids. Just in case.

*Silence.*

CAT. I thought you were just getting cold feet about me.

JAY. I can't do it.

*Beat.*

CAT. What are you saying?

*CAT tries once more to touch him. He pulls away. He picks up the suitcase.*

No – leave it. Put it down. We need to talk about this properly.

JAY. I'm serious, Cat. I can't do this. Please –

CAT. I want you to want to stay with me. I want you to trust me.

*Silence.*

Oh, fuck. Please say something.

*Silence. He shakes his head.*

JAY. I need to go.

CAT. We can't –

JAY. Please.

*Beat. He picks up the suitcase and exits. She stands silently as the door slams.*

**Scene Eight**

*1991. Late at night. The family home's living room. There are boxes stacked in a corner – suitcases packed. The record player is lying out on the floor.*

*A noise, like a scratching record.*

JAMIE *enters. He looks at the player. He upends a boxful of records. He looks at them, scattered all over the floor.*

*He methodically starts to break the records in half, one by one. The background noise becomes so loud it's deafening.*

**Scene Nine**

*2016. A quiet kitchen, somewhere that's not London.* SARAH, *now forty, is making tea.* JAY *sits at a table.*

SARAH. I've only got skimmed milk. Hope that's alright.

*She passes him a mug.*

You look so different.

JAY. Older, I expect.

SARAH. No. Not exactly.

*Beat.*

Fucking Facebook. Easy for someone to track you down these days. Should have told Mum when we moved – it won't be worth the bother twenty years from now, anyone can look me up.

JAY. Sorry. If it wasn't / appropriate –

SARAH. I'm joking.

*Beat.*

Sort of.

*Beat.*

What do you do now, then?

JAY. I work for an insurance company.

SARAH. Not a music journalist, like you planned?

JAY. Not quite.

SARAH. Not a teacher?

JAY. No.

*Beat.*

SARAH. What are you doing here, then?

JAY. I don't really know, to be honest.

*Beat.*

SARAH. You wanted to talk. You said it was important.

JAY. I think I just wanted to –

*Beat.*

See you. Sort of. See what happened to you.

SARAH. Your dad happened to me.

JAY. I meant, since then.

*Beat.*

SARAH. I've got kids now.

JAY. Have you?

SARAH. Two girls. Eight and five.

JAY. Wow.

SARAH. Their dad's not around any more. Left. But I've got a new fella. He's nice. Kind. I think kindness is underrated, you know.

JAY. Does he know?

SARAH. About your dad?

JAY. Yeah.

SARAH. Not yet.

One day, maybe.

*Beat.*

I'm careful about who I tell. I still feel like I have to be so careful. Even aged forty, even with a degree and a mortgage and two kids. Don't want to be the girl who seduced her teacher.

JAY. That's not what happened.

SARAH. You've changed your tune.

JAY. You were fifteen.

*Beat.*

What I said to you. Back then. It / was...

SARAH. You were fifteen.

JAY. Should have known better.

SARAH. We had to grow up fast, didn't we? You and me.

*Beat.*

You got kids?

*Beat.*

JAY. Not quite yet.

SARAH. One on the way?

JAY. In a couple of weeks.

SARAH. What's she like, your wife?

JAY. Not my wife. Girlfriend – or...

*Beat.*

It's hard to talk about Cat.

She's kind too. The kindest person I've ever met. And funny. And clever. And she always does the right thing, even when it's hard. Because she knows you should.

SARAH. Does she know?

*Beat.*

JAY. He's dying. My dad. It's the first time I've seen him in years. I had nothing to do with him – after.

SARAH. I don't want to know. I don't want to hear anything about him. Sorry.

JAY. Okay.

*Beat.*

SARAH. Did your friend Tom fancy me at school?

JAY. Was it obvious?

SARAH. Nobody ever fancied me. I used to think it was the glasses, or the fact my mum wouldn't let me roll my skirt up above knee-length or that she kept coming and picking me up from the school gates in her Volvo when everyone else could just get the bus. I wasn't like the girls in our year, not really.

And your dad told me that was why he liked me. Why I was special. Different. I was beautiful. I was too grown-up for the boys in our year. I fell for that, didn't I? I had this thing, something about me that nobody else had, that's what he said.

*Beat.*

He was right about that. I had him. Like some fucking rockstar everyone worshipped. Thing is about rockstars – they all die eventually, don't they? They turn back into sad old men in PE kits just wanting to be something different.

JAY. I'm sorry for what he did to you.

SARAH. Me too.

*Beat.*

JAY. When you have kids. When you become a parent. What changes?

*Beat.* SARAH *smiles.*

SARAH. Everything.

**Scene Ten**

*A café. 1991 and 2016. In both timeframes, 'Ashes to Ashes' is gently playing over a PA, barely audible.*

*In 1991,* TOM *sits at a table, alone.*

*In 2016,* SIAN *is taking her coat off, putting it over the back of a chair.*

*In 1991,* JAMIE *walks in.* TOM *looks up.*

TOM. Hi.

JAMIE. I haven't got long.

TOM. You're moving away. Sian said.

JAMIE. Van's coming this afternoon. I've got to help load it.

TOM. Where are you going?

JAMIE *shrugs.*

*In 2016, the bell on the café door rings as it opens.* CAT *enters.* SIAN *stands up.*

SIAN. Catherine?

CAT *looks down at her belly.*

CAT. Wonder what gave that away?

TOM. You don't know where you're going?

JAMIE. No, I'm saying you don't need to know.

*Silence.*

TOM. Why did you want to see me, then?

SIAN. Sit down. Can I get you something? Tea, or –

CAT. Water's fine.

SIAN *exits.*

JAMIE. I've got something for you.

*He puts a box on the table. After a beat,* TOM *opens it.*

SIAN *re-enters and places the water in front of* CAT.

SIAN. Here you go.

>*Beat.*

>Sorry. It's so weird to finally meet you.

>TOM *looks through the box.*

TOM. What is this?

JAMIE. Just some old magazines, cassettes, stuff like that.

TOM. All your *NME*s.

JAMIE. Yeah. Don't want them any more.

TOM. You've been collecting them for ages.

>JAMIE *shrugs.*

SIAN. When are you –

CAT. Three weeks.

SIAN. Do you know what you're / having?

CAT. Do you know where your brother is?

TOM. I can't take these.

JAMIE. They're going in the bin, then.

TOM. I thought you hated me?

JAMIE. I do. Just don't want them to go to waste.

>TOM *packs everything neatly back in the box.*

SIAN. He told me you didn't know. About Dad. Or any of it.

>That must have been... a shock.

CAT. That's a fucking understatement.

SIAN. I'm sorry. I feel like I started all of this.

CAT. No. You didn't.

TOM. Thanks.

>JAMIE *shrugs and gets up.*

SIAN. He was so young when it all happened. Fifteen.

CAT. He's a grown-up now, though, isn't he?

JAMIE. Bye.

SIAN. It's hard to explain. If you saw him and Dad when he was growing up... I mean, look, Dad definitely had a favourite and it wasn't me.

CAT. You should tell your brother I'll do this on my own if I need to.

If you see him.

TOM. Is that it, then?

CAT. Are you seeing him?

SIAN. Dad's not going to wake up now, I don't think. I've tried to get him to come to the hospital.

JAMIE. Yep. That's it.

CAT. I'm sorry.

TOM. We're not even going to keep in touch, or –

JAMIE. Why?

SIAN. Why are you sorry?

CAT. It's what you say, isn't it? I don't know.

*JAMIE turns to leave.*

TOM. I've got nobody else. Not really.

SIAN. I've got nobody. Don't speak to Jay now, not really. Mum's gone. Dad – this isn't even the end of Dad, really. That happened a long time ago.

CAT. I can't imagine not having any family.

SIAN. I turned out alright.

JAMIE. I'm sorry. It's just better if we – don't.

New start, yeah? You'll make other friends.

*Silence.*

Loads of people lose touch, it's not a big deal.

*Beat.*

See ya.

TOM. Jamie?

CAT. You're not what I expected.

*Beat.* JAMIE *stops.*

JAMIE. Take care of the stuff, yeah.

JAMIE *exits.* TOM *stares at the box.*

CAT. I'm sorry for both of you. I bet it's horrible, having to grow up like that.

*Beat.*

But this is nothing to do with her. It's not. He has to stop running away. He can't be half-in and half-out. I can't stop her from growing up without a dad, but I'm never going to let her feel the difference if we do it by ourselves. Do you understand?

SIAN. Yeah.

*Beat.* TOM *picks up the box and exits.*

It's my dad's favourite. This song.

CAT. My parents are huge Bowie fans.

SIAN. You know he slept with a fourteen-year-old, right? David Bowie. I read about it the other day. I mean, I'm not surprised. They all did, didn't they? That's just what it was like. A sign of the times. It's all rock and roll, isn't it?

*Beat.*

Weird though. I've had so many conversations about him – everyone's sad but nobody talks about that. Even if they know about it. And it's a big thing. It should be a big thing, right?

CAT *doesn't reply.* SIAN *gives her a business card.*

CAT. What's this?

SIAN. My number.

CAT. I'm serious, Sian. He might not come back.

SIAN. Doesn't matter. You call me for anything. Any time. Alright?

*CAT puts the card in her bag.*

I never actually thought I'd be good with kids. Do you know that? Didn't ever think I'd hear from Jamie again, not really – and I'm not the maternal type myself. I decided years ago. People ask why sometimes and I don't really know. Could be what happened. Might just be how I'm wired.

*Beat.*

She's lucky, you know. Having you as a mum.

*She tentatively hugs CAT. After a beat, CAT hugs her back.*

Take care.

## Scene Eleven

*2016. A hospital room, again. Everything is quiet. Still. It's almost jarring.*

MARTIN *lies in a bed – peaceful, calm. The hat is still on his head.* SIAN *sleeps on a plastic chair in the corner, curled up into the seat.* JAY *sits beside* MARTIN.

JAY. My first memory is of Camber Sands. I'm two. I'm racing you on a beach, sort of seeing water glint in the distance. It's the sea, but I don't know that yet. It's just shapes and feeling and sensation. The sand is under my feet and it's hitting the soles hard where I don't have my balance right. You're ahead of me shouting 'Race you! C'mon, Jamie, race you!' and I'm wobbling my way towards you in the distance just ahead of me. I fall over and you catch me. Remember?

*Beat.*

I spent a long time really wanting to be you, and worrying that I wouldn't be.

*Beat.*

When I had my first date with Cat my favourite thing about her was her laugh. That made me want to see her again, even though she had to keep on at me to take her out the first time. I'm bad at dating – or being with people, to be honest – but not her. When she laughs it sounds like a proper cackle. It's not a girly laugh or a sexy laugh, it's a sort of – when she laughs at you, really laughs, she means it. Head thrown back, belly-shaking sort of means it. I know when she says she loves me, she means it. When she says I'm a good person – she was the only person who could say that and I'd sort of believe they meant it, sometimes.

I didn't believe anyone else. Not after you. Maybe not even before you. I don't know. I was never – good. I couldn't be.

I don't want to be like you. I don't know how to be like you anyway, even if I tried. There is no blueprint for being a dad. You didn't leave me one.

I'm here now. Is that what you wanted?

*Silence.* MARTIN*'s breathing has slowed.*

I'm five and we're at a football match and the air smells like autumn. You lift me onto your shoulders so I can see the players running round after a goal. I'm twelve and we're having a bonfire and you're making Mum jump by pretending you've burnt yourself every time you chuck a twig on. I'm thirteen and listening to you putting on Bowie in the car and you don't let me just fast-forward and skip ahead to the songs I like because then, you say, you miss bits. I'm fifteen and in a new place in the countryside that Mum's up and moved us to and you're not there. I've asked my old friends to forget about me. I change my name. I tell her and Sian it's easier to pretend you've never existed but that's not true, is it?

*Silence. He looks at* MARTIN.

Dad?

*Silence.* CAT *enters, behind him. He doesn't notice until she puts a hand on his shoulder.*

**Scene Twelve**

*2016. The Bowie wall in Brixton.*

JAY *sits on a bench with* CAT, *him sipping a takeaway coffee, her holding a bottle of water. They're both dressed in black clothes – smartly.*

JAY. It's bigger than you'd think.

CAT. I know.

*He offers her the coffee.*

Can't. Not supposed to.

JAY. Shit. Of course. / Sorry.

CAT. Don't be. I kept forgetting at first. Kept buying myself double-shot lattes and having to pour them down the sink at work.

*He laughs.*

JAY. I didn't know that.

CAT. I've missed you.

JAY. I'm sorry.

CAT. Good.

JAY. I'm glad you came.

CAT. I'm glad you did.

*He reaches over and takes her hand.*

JAY. Is this okay?

*She doesn't reply, but holds his hand back.*

CAT. How are you?

JAY. I thought I'd feel – different. I don't know.

CAT. Different how?

JAY. Just, freer. Or something.

Like something would be over. New chapter, blank slate.

CAT. A dad is a dad. That doesn't change.

JAY. That's true.

*Beat.*

CAT. Maybe it's not true. I don't know.

*She puts his hand on the bump.*

*Beat.*

JAY. I'm really scared. You know that, right?

CAT. You and me both, mate. Babies are scary. Kids are scary. Anyone who says they're born ready for parenthood is a fucking liar.

*Beat.*

I've always been scared too, even if you haven't seen it.

*Beat.*

There's so much, isn't there. The planet. Global warming. The economy. Neighbourhoods, schools, whether she'll make friends that'll be nice to her. If she'll be healthy. And all of that – that's before we even start hoping that she just gets the best bits of you and me. But she's her own person. Unique as a fingerprint. None of the things we've done are on her. New chapter, blank slate. Yeah?

*Silence.*

JAY. I can't believe how many flowers are still here.

CAT. It's lovely.

JAY. Do you think anyone's going to remember him?

CAT. What, Bowie? Yeah, probably.

*Beat. He isn't sure if she's serious, just for a second – but then laughs.*

I'm being silly. I know what you mean.

JAY. I don't want it to be just me.

CAT. Nah. It won't be.

JAY. Good.

*She leans her head on his shoulder. Lights fade.*

**Scene Thirteen**

CAT *and* JAY*'s flat. 2019.*

CAT *is putting birthday cards around the space. There are presents wrapped in the corner.* JAY *is trying to blow up a balloon.*

*She laughs at him.*

CAT. You look ridiculous.

JAY. Thanks.

CAT. Where's the cake?

JAY. Fridge.

CAT. I'll get the candles now.

> *She exits.* JAY *finishes blowing up the balloon.*

> (*Offstage.*) Did you make this?

JAY. Why?

CAT (*offstage*). Since when do you bake?

JAY. I've got hidden talents.

CAT (*offstage*). Mum and Dad aren't coming till later. I thought you were just going to pick up a Colin the Caterpillar or something.

JAY. I've got one of those as well. Bottom drawer.

> CAT *re-enters with a homemade cake.*

CAT. You've got two cakes for six of us?

JAY. I want her to remember it. I remember my third birthday. At least I think I do. Do you?

CAT. Definitely not.

> *The doorbell goes. Both jump.*

JAY. Shit – I told her to call when she was outside. I said don't ring the bell.

CAT. We need to wake her up soon anyway.

JAY. Even so.

CAT. You're an overprotective git, do you know that?

JAY. Fine, I'll get it then, shall I?

> JAY *exits*. CAT *looks at the room around her. She straightens a couple of cards. Everything is perfect.*

> JAY *re-enters with* SIAN.

SIAN. My phone died.

JAY. You could just like – softly knock.

SIAN. It's a party, isn't the birthday girl meant to be awake?

CAT. Any minute now.

> CAT *hugs* SIAN *tightly.*

> Give me your coat. This is lovely, where's this from?

SIAN. Don't go out and buy one.

CAT. Alright, I'm not about to copy.

SIAN. No, I mean I've got you one for your birthday. Don't buy one. It took me bloody ages to decide what to get you.

JAY. You got me nose-hair trimmers for my birthday.

SIAN. Yeah, and it looks like they've been a great success. You're welcome.

> CAT *laughs.*

> Right. Prosecco. Shall I put this in the fridge?

JAY. It's a kids' birthday party, Sian.

SIAN. Exactly.

> SIAN *exits for the kitchen.*

JAY. Hey.

> CAT *looks at him.*

> I love you.

CAT. I know.

*A sudden cry comes from a baby monitor in the corner. They both turn around.* SIAN *re-enters.*

SIAN. Sounds like the guest of honour's awake, then.

CAT. Here we go. Ready?

*She heads in the direction of the bedroom.* JAY *stops her.*

JAY. No, it's alright. I'll go.

JAY *exits. As the noise from the baby monitor begins to quieten, with* JAY *gently shushing their daughter,* CAT *lights the birthday candles.*

*The End.*

**www.nickhernbooks.co.uk**

 facebook.com/nickhernbooks

twitter.com/nickhernbooks